Thank you for joining
me on my journey

Reviews

Just finished your book!

I absolutely LOVED it! The words seemed to speak directly to me. Each chapter gave me just what I was needing at that time. I feel motivated and encouraged to continue on my enlightened path knowing that I am supported and that the people & experiences will appear at the exact right time to help guide me …. Just like you have Daphne

Chantal Lapierre

What a beautiful and deeply inspiring story! Daphne is such a bright light on earth. Her journey is filled with deep lessons that show us that no matter what happens we can choose to thrive. She is a true example of someone who purposely chooses to live a life of gratitude and this has blessed her in so many ways. This is a wonderful read for everyone, especially those feeling like life is challenging them. This is a story of magic that speaks to the soul of the reader.

Ginette Biro

Daphne's journey is a testament that when tragedy occurs there can be an amazing journey of healing and new life. I have had the pleasure of knowing Daphne for 22 years and watch her grow and heal. This book was like having a conversation with her about what she has tried and what she has learned. Keep on with your Journey of you and keep us all informed.

Nancy W

Cover Design: 2021 Kostas Koukouzikis

You Do You

Daphne McDonagh

Cover Design
Konstantinos Koukouzikis

Wand Publishing
Edmonton, Alberta, Canada

www.wandpublishing.ca

First edition 2021
ISBN: 978-17777437-1-0

Published by Wand Publishing
www.wandpublishing.ca

Dedication

I dedicate this book to:

My Parents, Arnold and Brenda Dietrich

Thank you for never giving up on me.

Even in the darkest of moments, when no one else believed I would live.

My Husband and Life-Long Partner

Doug McDonagh for being my biggest advocate and supporter in following my passions wherever they take me in being the light that I came back here to be.

Our Son

Koltin McDonagh for choosing us to be your parents in this lifetime.

I am forever grateful for how you inspire me to choose to be my authentic self.

Contents

Preface and Acknowledgments

I would like to give a heartfelt thank you to everyone in my life that has contributed to allowing me to be my true and authentic self.

I understand the time is now for me to write this book. Even after years of talking myself out of it, I realize that in order for me to live my truth and walk my talk, it is time for me to share what I have learned in my life. If the world is a reflection of my thoughts on all levels and the people in my life are reflecting my thoughts back to me, then I need to step up my game to be open to my deepest wisdom.

Thank you Ginette Biro for inspiring me to share the gift of my story with others.

Cynthia Gauvreau from Wand Publishing for walking with me on this life-changing experience.

And, I especially would like to send out a Big Thank You to the magical individuals who walked with me on this journey to get the words out.

At times, this process felt scary like I was climbing a mountain without a map. I had no idea what I was doing, but as I chose not to give up and keep moving forward my fear subsided and I began to see the light at the end of the tunnel.

I also would like to send out a huge thank you to the many others who have helped me along the way.

Forward

When I asked her how she talked to angels, she shrugged her shoulders and told me she simply got out of her own way and listened. I couldn't understand how someone could be so happy. I've always wanted to know why life was so hard and I needed to know the process for healing.

We are so different yet so much alike. I am the proverbial skeptic. Daphne is the optimal optimist. My quest for knowledge is insatiable. I discovered that magick can't be learned, it has to be embraced. We made a great team and our friendship blossomed as we learned from each other. We learned that the thoughts, beliefs, and memories we had; including our jobs, our bank balances, and all of the relationships are all in our past.

Daphne taught me that I had to let go. Together we learned that every event was a part of our story, but that it was not us. It was so freeing for both of us to see that each day a new cycle began. Daphne reminded me that it was safe for me to be me. I taught her that feelings were the core of recovery. Recover Your Joy was created from our friendship.

With new beginnings we encouraged each other to use our minds, connect with our hearts and align ourselves with our true purpose of divine will. Angels are everywhere, ready, waiting, and willing to help us. There are so many powerful Archangels. One of our favourites is Metatron who reminds us that each morning it is time for us to step into our true authenticity and higher selves.

Daphne is one of those special angels whose love and light will touch you. You will be blessed as she reminds you that healing happens when you embrace the beautiful light in each day with gratitude.

Nancy Nance Chaplin

CHAPTER 1 The Early Years

Life is magical when we open our hearts and our minds to the infinite possibilities surrounding us. I am beginning to understand the vastness of my journey and I have only cracked the surface. There are no words in the English language that I can use to explain how it feels when I think about the abundance of knowledge that I was blessed to receive while being bathed in the Rainbow Colors by the beloved Rainbow Council.

The further I go on my journey, the more I am seeing that everyone is unique and Spirit is an all-encompassing Being. I see how each and every one of us is unique when we are open to listening, and how some people are blessed to see pictures in their mind's eye that play out like a movie reel, while others are blessed to hear the messages directly. I have learned that my mind starts hearing songs to help me translate the messages being shared with me.

I am aware there are many different religions and faiths on this earthly plane, and I honor those who have travelled the world studying the many different forms. I will be the first to admit that I am no guru and I will never claim to be. For the purpose of keeping things congruent throughout the story, I am choosing to use the words 'Spirit' and 'Universe'.

Please allow me to share a little backstory with you to help you understand where I am coming from. Looking back, I feel so blessed to have chosen the parents that I did.

I am so happy and grateful that my parents allowed me to try as many things as I did when I was young. Even when they knew I wouldn't be able to actually do what I thought I wanted to do, they would let me try whether I succeeded or not.

A very valuable lesson that I learned early on, was to try different things and keep moving forward. As long as I did the best I could at whatever I was doing, life would only get better and better.

I remember when I was under ten years old that we had a skating rink right across the street from our house. I would go skating every day. Oh boy, let me tell you, I wasn't very good in the beginning at all. I had so many bumps and bruises but I always got back up and kept going.

From a very young age, I would spend my summers in Lloydminster with my Grandma and Grandpa Dietrich. They were my dad's parents. I have fond memories of touring Alberta and Saskatchewan with my grandparents. We would pack up their campervan and go. I think that is where my sense of adventure started. We spent many hours on the road singing songs and talking about the new places we would visit and the new things we would get to see and experience.

This was long before digital cameras were even thought of and I am forever grateful my grandmother took as many pictures as she did. She was a very crafty lady. Come to think of it, that is probably where my craftiness came from too. Every year she would make me a fancy cloth-covered album with pictures from all of our summer adventures.

My Grandma Dietrich was an amazing lady who taught me many valuable lessons, even though I may not have realized it at the time. She was such a talented lady who did so many amazing things. She was an amazing seamstress and made me a new dress every summer that I visited. She loved to paint ceramics; she had an entire room filled to the brim with everything you could think of to do with ceramics. She was also an amazing cake decorator and patchwork quilt maker.

Every summer we would come back from our travels with fresh fruit that we would need to can. She made the best cinnamon buns. Every year she would win awards at the local fair for the amazing patchwork blankets she created.

I never could figure out where she found time to complete all of these tasks, but I am forever grateful for her teaching me the value of hard work.

I was also blessed to be able to spend time with my cousins. My dad's sister also lived in Lloydminster and she had two daughters that were a little older than me. My Aunt Elenor also ran a dayhome so there were always kids to play with. We went on many adventures, building forts and constructing castles to ward off the dragons that were surrounding the moat! Looking back now, I am grateful for the sense of family this instilled in me.

Grandpa Dietrich would take me for a drive and we would often end up at the local mini-golf course. It was so cute how he would nap in the truck while I played. His quiet, calm state of being always let me know that I was loved. I am so grateful for everything he did to support me when I was visiting.

There was also this very cool museum we used to go to all the time. The best way I can describe it is to say it was like the movie, *Night at the Museum*. There were statues and stuffed animals. I would pretend they were talking to me too. Years later when *Night at the Museum* came to theaters it was fun watching it. I kinda felt like I helped create the movie even though I had nothing to do with it.

While we were living in Regina we were out at my mom's parent's house almost every day. I got to run around the farm. In the garden, I watched all of the amazing plants grow and learned about life and how the cows and chickens became the food in the freezer. There were many years where I assisted with the butchering of the harvested animals. I am very blessed to have had that experience, especially being a city kid who was completely country at heart.

Growing up, I learned that if there was someone in need and we could help them, we did. During harvest, I spent many nights at the farm while my parents helped my grandparents get the crops off of the field.

It was normal for us to be over at the neighbours and for them to be at our place too. I remember the nights when I was really little and there was so much noise coming from the kitchen because the grown-ups were playing cards and laughing so loud that I couldn't get to sleep. They played everything from *Canasta* to *Poker.* If it was a card game, my parents knew how to play it.

There was always an abundance of what we needed and we always shared what we had with others. I was truly blessed as a child to not worry about where my next meal would come from. I was always grateful to get the bags of hand-me-down clothes from my cousins who were a few years older than me. It was like Christmas during every season in my house.

'Sharing is caring' is a motto I still live by today.

Even when we moved to the new province of Alberta, the sense of community was very strong in my life. We landed in Calahoo which was a small town that had one main road and a general store where everyone knew everyone, and if anyone needed anything we always knew someone would lend a hand.

My dad still lives by that motto today, if the neighbour calls and needs a hand, he's the first one to jump in his truck and be there. I think it used to bother my mom at how much my dad was always willing to help the neighbours out, but looking back now, we never lacked anything ever. OK, well maybe we did at some point, but I never knew it.

Please understand, I did not have things handed to me whenever I wanted them, I had to work for anything extra that I thought I needed.

The one thing I recall working hard for was a 'Billy Cook' barrel racing saddle. For people who do not live in the world of horses or know anything about what is required to raise a horse and have the appropriate gear to go riding, please allow me to try and explain. I had to save, I think it was, $700 dollars for the saddle, and for a pre-teen girl, that felt like $7000.

I did extra chores like shoveling the barn, cleaning the house, and mowing the big half-acre lawn, which was our front yard. It probably wasn't a full half-acre, but the push-mower made it seem like it. I am pretty sure my parents helped me out more than I know to reach the $700 dollar goal. I really felt so blessed to have this saddle.

I had to make sure the animals were always taken care of first. My chores needed to be done for the horses before I got to eat or I was given the privilege to go riding and off to my other sports activities. I am so grateful for the lessons I was learning about responsibility at the time without even realizing it.

I was a busy and active kid. I am really glad that labels didn't exist when I was a child because I would have been given a list of them. I was that 'Chatty Cathy' in the back of the classroom always turning to talk to my neighbour to ask what was going on.

It wasn't until many years later, and many life-changing experiences later, that I learned what ADHD really stood for:

Attention Dialed into a Higher Dimension.

I was also blessed to never have been labeled with any disability while I was in school. However, teachers had a difficult time dealing with me in their classes. I was always the one talking out of turn and causing a ruckus. There were many times that I was kicked out into the hall so that I would not disturb the rest of the class.

Just because some may not understand where I am coming from, does not mean it is wrong. There are always different ways to accomplish the same task. To this day, I love the phrase, "You wouldn't ask a fish to climb a tree, would you ?" As I work my way through the process of writing, I realize how blessed I truly am to have experienced so many things.

How many times have you beaten yourself up because you thought you were not good enough? When really, there was nothing wrong at all. You were simply not using your skills and abilities that were your strong points. So many times in my life I was told that I had too much energy, so I did what I thought I needed to do to make myself seem smaller.

I always liked to do things differently than most. I thank the Universe that my parents raised me to be a strong and independent person. Like the time when I was seven or eight and thought it would be a grand idea to ride my bike down a big hill on a gravel road without a bike helmet. Let's be real for a moment, I do not even remember there being such a thing as bike helmets when I was young. There is still a scar on my left shin to prove I survived.

Pause for a moment. How many times have you done something, that looking back now, you realize may not have been such a grand idea? I feel blessed to now know these were the best experiences of my life. Had I not rode that bike down the hill, I may have never learned it really wasn't such a great idea after all. I was beginning to understand what the phrase hindsight is 20/20 really meant.

I remember when we lived in Regina our address was on a corner at 1403 Brown Street. To this day, it still makes me chuckle because the house was actually forest green. I remember we had a CB tower attached to the side of our house. One Halloween, my dad dressed up in a gorilla costume and was climbing up and down the tower while he ran around on the roof. The neighbourhood kids thought it was wonderful. Even though I did not realize it at the time, this lesson from my father taught me it was perfectly ok to be who I am, just the way I was.

In Regina, we had a big black corner fireplace on the left-hand side of the living room. I recall how I would pretend it was the great fireplace in my castle and how the fire was protecting me. You can ask my parents, there were many a night I fell asleep laying in front of it too.

Funny how some of our memories are the stories our parents tell over and over. Like the one about my first day of kindergarten. I was climbing on the jungle gym that was in the classroom and I thought it would be super fun to hang upside down on the monkey bars. It did not matter to me that I was wearing a pretty green dress that my grandmother had made for me. It was all about having fun and that was all that mattered to me.

I was surprised by how they reacted. I thought I was doing something super awesome being able to hang upside down like that. Apparently, it wasn't socially acceptable ….. And so, the lessons continued. I was five and completely unaware of socially acceptable standards, but that is what life is about…..Learning and growing.

Think back to when you were young ……. What was the first lesson you learned and how has it continued to affect you in your life?

CHAPTER 2 School Days

My family and I were blessed to be surrounded by so many amazing people in our lives. I remember the day Jack Grad asked me if I had any money with me. I didn't know why he was asking, but I reached deep into my sweet little pocket and pulled out a dollar. We walked out to the barn together and he gave me a choice of 3 different baby horses; two colts and a filly. For those of you that do not know, a colt is a baby boy and a filly is a baby girl.

Please allow me to give you a little back story on Jack Grad. He and his wife, Shirley, along with their sons, ran a PMU (Pregnant Mare Urine) barn. They were some of the kindest people I knew. Being a city kid that was at the farm almost every day I did not think that there was anything weird about this as it was explained to me that they were catching the pee. The Pregnant Mare Urine or PMU Industry produces pharmaceuticals containing the urine of impregnated horses.

Many of the mares would have their babies while there. Jack knew how much I liked horses so he sold me a Red Roan colt. He reminded me of an orange sunset, so I called him Buck! I thought it was a clever name. We had him for many years and he was the best horse ever. My parents helped me saddle him because I was too short to reach, but Buck was a great way for me to begin to learn about being responsible.

When I was in grade four we moved from Saskatchewan to Alberta. From the Big city of Regina to the small town of Calahoo. Calahoo had one main road, a general store, a hockey arena, and some ball diamonds. This was the sort of place, that if you were born here, there was either a ball glove or hockey stick placed in your hand (depending on the season). These were the local gathering places, and if you wanted to be a part of something you had better be willing to learn a sport. My mom loved ball, and I remember one year she did a great job of coaching a little league team.

I tried very hard, but ball was not my forte. Yes, it was a drastic change, but seeing as I was only roughly 10 years old when we did that, I didn't feel like it was that big of a deal.

I was excited that I was going to live in the same place as my horse Buck (the red roan) and that I would get to see him every day. What I didn't realize was all the extra work I was going to need to do. It was ok because after I was done with my chores, I got to go riding and that made me feel so free like I could take on the world. Everyone was so welcoming. People cared and it showed.

I went to Camilla, the nearest school to where I lived. It was kindergarten to grade 9. I went from walking to school every day to having to ride the bus for 45 minutes each way in the morning and at night. It really was wonderful as I would get to visit with my friends and we would plan out what we were going to do after school.

My grade 6 teacher was Mr. Soetart, he was my all-time favorite teacher. He challenged me to learn more and reach higher. He walked with me as I learned how to be me. I remember him catching me being "bad" one time. I was standing by the big black tire on the playground while some of the other kids were smoking. I was guilty by association, so I got suspended too. This was a valuable lesson that I didn't necessarily learn at the time. A lesson about how you are the sum of the 5 people you spend the most time with. This one seemed to have been a lesson I kept learning over and over again.

In junior high, we got to pick options and I felt like it was the first time (in school) that I had a choice. I was so grateful for the school counselor, Miss Budzack. She helped me many times. As I matured, I learned not only the value of hard work to become a great athlete but also, how to speak my truth.

I discovered my love for music and learned how to play the bass clarinet. Mr. Newton was the best. In my mind, he was the coolest teacher. He fed my desire to learn and grow and we even put together a wood-wind quartet with three of my in-school best friends - Stacey, Tara, and Shaussica.

I loved sports! I loved spending time with the people who made me feel good.

Competing in rodeos as a junior barrel racer gave me so much - a job, responsibility, maturity, and incredible joy. The rodeo family was a very tight-knit community. If ever anyone needed anything, there was always someone there to lend a hand.

My grade 8 teacher was Mrs. Ferguson. At the Halloween dance, I dressed up as a rodeo clown. This was my best costume ever, except that time in kindergarten when my mom dressed me up as Minnie Mouse. Before this, I had always thought dressing up was stupid.

I never really had or have been one for costumes. I didn't know why I needed to pretend to be someone I am not. As I look back now, it really doesn't surprise me that I am the person I am. All of the little things that I did when I was younger really have set me up for the person I am today.

In grade 9, I was on the grad committee. I helped organize and put together the event that brought us all together to celebrate our accomplishments. Bringing people together fills my heart with so much joy. I love connecting good people with good people for the greater good.

What in your life fills your heart with joy?

CHAPTER 3 Comforts

The summer of 1992 is the summer I will never forget as long as I am here on earth. My horse Echo and I were finally working together magically in the LRA (Lake Land) and WRA (Wild Rose) Rodeo Associations. I felt like I was on top of the world. My dad was team roping with Lyle. He and his nephew Dusty were traveling the Alberta Rodeo circuit with us. He was a junior bull rider, so this meant that he rode steers, not actual full-sized bulls. I had such a crush on Dusty. He had the softest, bluest eyes and a crooked smile that made my heart sing. I was sure that we were going to fall in love and spend the rest of our lives together. You need to know, I was 15 years old at the time and I thought I knew everything. Dusty was so shy and quiet, it was awesome seeing as I always liked to talk.

It was a sunny day at the Smoky Lake Rodeo and I was on top of the world. I remember it like it was yesterday. Dusty made a point to come over to say, "Have a good run" before my turn in the barrel racing competition. That was the first time he ever did that and I was over the moon with excitement. Echo and I completed an amazing run and I felt like I was having the best day of my life.

I really wanted to show some support to him too because this was the first day ever that he was entering the actual bull riding competition.

I remember crawling up the side of the arena fence so I could get a good view of what was happening. I wish I would have known then what I know now, maybe it would have made seeing him smash his head on the back of the bull's hump and being stomped on by the bull, a little easier to swallow.

As always, everyone came together to support one another. My dad even did the eulogy at his funeral. I was not able to be there in body, but I was totally there in spirit. I was told it was standing room only. He was an awesome guy so that doesn't surprise me.

Dusty and I were Twin Flames and we have shared many past lives together.

Some believe a twin flame relationship is when two people are perfectly matched as a result of shared pain or another difficulty. Others believe a twin flame is an intense soul connection, sometimes called a "mirror soul," thought to be a person's other half. It is based on the idea that sometimes one soul gets split into two bodies.

The important part is in the dynamics between the two people and it's where the difference between a twin flame and a life partner (or soulmate) really exists. So, being twin flames did not mean that we were supposed to live a long and happy life together. One of the main characteristics of a twin flame relationship is it will be both challenging and healing.

I discovered that in our last shared past life, I left first. In this lifetime, it was his exit that led me to meet my soulmate. I continued to compete in rodeos for the rest of the summer and ended up being season leader in the Wild Rose Association.

Grade 10 had just started and I was a guppy just learning how to swim in the pond of what was High School. I was really grateful Miss Budzack (the counselor) had come from Camilla to the high school as well. I felt safe and like nothing could stop me.

I was making friends easily and playing volleyball. I was even blessed to be asked to be a part of the Alberta Volleyball team. I was the youngest on the team and loved every minute of it. I really felt like I had the world by the tail. I was loving life and all of my new adventures. Two months into grade 10 and I was doing alright passing all of my classes when suddenly everything changed.

My Grandma Gottselig, from my mom's side, had been visiting us. As she was leaving Sunday morning, she looked at me, and pointed, and said, "You Be Careful." Years passed before I found out that she knew something was going to happen, she just didn't know what.

She thought I was going to get hurt in a riding accident, little did she know the magnitude of her statement.

Who or what in your life has made you feel safe?

CHAPTER 4 The Journey Begins

October 27th, 1992 was the day I said goodbye to my innocent exuberance and embarked on a lifelong journey to become the being that I was born to be.

My mother and I were involved in a near-fatal car accident with a large delivery truck on our way home from a volleyball game. The doctors did not think I would survive after the massive closed-head brain injury I sustained when I was thrown from the car.

My mom tells me I was being my regular chatty Cathy and telling her a story as we were driving and I just stopped talking mid-sentence. She went to look over at me to see why I stopped talking and then she felt the impact.

Call it whatever you want, God, Spirit, Universal Consciousness, but I believe I was pulled from the car so that I did not get more physically hurt and I could choose to stay here to help others.

All the angels were looking after me. From surviving the accident, to the moment that my Dad said "No" when the doctors asked him if they could harvest my organs once he got to the hospital.

The doctors told my dad I was going to be a vegetable for the rest of my life "If I did survive." From what I have been told, his response was, "Then she will be my vegetable." It took my dad years to tell my mom what the doctors said that night.

My dad did not care if I was a vegetable. All that mattered to him was I was here with my family. My prognosis was guarded due to the neurological injuries I sustained.

I am so grateful my family and friends never gave up on me. I have a whole new respect and understanding of how loved I was.

I can only imagine the challenges my parents went through to stay in the hospital for two weeks-day and night, to make sure that someone was always with me and holding my hand, while I was on life support. They believed the connection was necessary for me. I am so grateful they did that for me.

My Dad would take the night shift and stay up with me, telling me stories and holding my hand. He told me that my vitals would go up when he came to my hospital room door. It was like I knew his presence and felt safe when he was around. Even though the doctors did not have a positive outlook for me, my family knew differently.

My Mom's Sister, Gloria, who lived in the neighbouring province to us, did distant color/light therapy on me from her home. She told me when I was in the hospital she

put colored glass over a picture of me to help increase my healing vibrations while it sat in the sunlight.

Gloria would test every day to see what color I was at. When I asked her how she tested, she explained "In order to check, I held your picture in one hand and had a pendulum in the other hand. I would put various colored glass over your pic one at a time and ask if this color was the level you were at.

Once the pendulum said yes then I would know where you were at - red. I then put an orange glass over the picture and set it in direct sunlight. Once the pendulum said orange was stronger, I changed the glass to the next one higher on the list. The pendulum said you were Red so I started with Orange to raise your level of consciousness."

Gloria always chose the color that was one level higher than where I was at, in order to pull my conscience level back up towards normal until I was awake and out of my coma.

Auntie Gloria told me "Every day I would test to see what color you were at, if it matched the color of the glass I would then put the next color on you. If you were not up there yet, I would leave that particular color for another day." The color levels went red, orange, yellow, green, blue, indigo.

I also learned that my Aunt Gloria sent sound tapes corresponding to the colors to be used in the same way. Mom played those for me while she was doing the corresponding color therapy on me. There was one for each color. Each one was about 30 minutes. It is amazing how color, light, and sound can be used interchangeably.

This procedure can be used for any type of illness. My Aunt Gloria told me, generally by the time the person is between green and blue, they are well on the way back

What have you done to heal in your life?

CHAPTER 5 Coming Together

Unless you too have experienced a traumatic brain injury, the sheer hell and suffering of my particular disability is unexplainable. It has been many years since the actual accident. I don't even want to imagine the pain and suffering my parents went through. I am their only and eldest daughter. My younger brother JJ, who is eleven years younger than me, was only 4 years old at the time. I'm certain he found everything to be very confusing and didn't know what was going on. It would have seemed that he had a really long sleepover at the babysitters as my parents were with me at the hospital.

My mom went home to be with my brother after I was removed from life support, but my parents ensured there was always someone with me while I recovered at the Royal Alex Hospital for two months.

There was so much support for me and my family. My mom couldn't keep up with writing a list of all the people who were coming to visit. She finally decided to get a book for everyone to write in when they were there. I am grateful she chose to hang onto it and give it to me years later so I am able to look back on the notes to see how far I really have come.

It is great being able to look back and see my incredible recovery and all the amazing people who came just to see me. It warms my heart to see how many people came together to support me and my family through this tragedy. It makes me think, why does there need to be a tragedy to bring people together? What if we could spread love as quickly as we spread tragedy, hate, and negativity, what an amazing world we would live in?

As I type this section, I want to look through and find out what day it was that the doctors took out the breathing tube.

The first note I read was from eight days after my injury and it said, "Dear Daffy, Well, you've always been a scrapper and you've always loved a challenge. You have one now and I expect you will meet it with the same determination you have met any challenges in the past. I came to visit to tell you not to rush too fast. Take your time and do it right. For once your stubborn disposition and hard head will serve you well. I never thought I'd ever say that. Hang in there."

Love Ray Soetaert

Please allow me to remind you that Mr. Soetaert was my Grade 6 teacher who made a huge impact on my life years before. Ray's note in my memory book reminded me of my persistence and tenacity.

I am truly grateful my body and mind held off on allowing me to consciously remember the worst of the accident and the earliest days of healing. I know that I heard everything people said around me. I am still dealing with deep-seated subconscious beliefs from hearing, "She is not going to pull through."

There was no way I was going to accept anyone telling me the words, "I was not going to recover." As they say, there is always another layer and just when I think I am good, something else pops up.

Before my accident, I was a very competitive athletic fifteen-year-old girl and when I was told that I couldn't do something, I would say, "Watch Me."

I was playing both high school and provincial level volleyball, as well as having just come off a very successful Rodeo season. I rode my horse twice a day, every day. You would never find me sitting still, I was always busy doing something.

The doctors really didn't have much hope that I would recover. They didn't feel there was any brain activity going on but my parents knew there was.

My mom and dad were there 24/7 and they noticed certain things I was doing. The doctors only came to see me in the morning and at night.

One morning my mom asked to make sure she was in the room when the doctor came to see me because she wanted me to show him I did have brain activity. On about day 10 after my injury, when the doctor came into the room, Mom said to me "Okay Daphne this is the guy you got to show, please lift your finger."

I actually remember lifting my finger for the doctor and seeing them both cry. Please remember, I was still in my coma at the time. This is the first and only memory I have after the accident, while I was still in a coma. I am grateful I chose to remember this pivotal moment of my healing recovery because it showed how much belief my parents had in me to prove to the doctors I was stronger than they thought.

As I look through the books with all of the notes from everyone, my heart is filled with so much joy. I found a note from my Grandma G, my mom's mom wrote. The one that told me to "Be Careful." She said, "I have sat with you for the past 10 days watching and praying for your healing process. Your Guardian Angels are watching over you and God is taking care of you. Who could ask for more? I'm going home in a day or two so keep up the good work and I will be back up to help look after you when you get home!! Grandpa finds it hard to express how he feels. He Loves you tooooo."

One of my major tasks on my healing journey was to remove the breathing apparatus so I could breathe on my own. The first attempt, 10 days after my injury, did not go so well because my lung collapsed. When I was finally able to have the tubes removed, 14 days after my injury, my breathing was shallow and labored because of the length of time that I required intubation.

Who is in your community that lifts you higher?

CHAPTER 6 Believe

Four days after being moved from ICU, my Grandma Dietrich, from my father's side came to see me and asked if there were any further signs of movement. I found her note from the book.

Dear Precious Daphne,

I just had to come this weekend again and I am so glad I did. You opened your eyes and smiled at grandma and even stuck out your tongue. I Love you.

She said "Daphne it's time to open your eyes", I didn't listen to her the first time, as a usual teenage girl does, but in grandma fashion, she looked at me and said again, "Daphne open your eyes!" Not wanting to disappoint her, I slightly opened both of my brown eyes to look at her.

It definitely wasn't like what you see on T.V. when people wake up and start asking what was happening. I think I already knew what was going on because Mom told me the nurses did an excellent job of telling me everything that was going on around me. I do not remember that day, I've just been told the story so many times that I can recite it as I remember. I can only imagine how excited everyone was as tears of joy were flowing when I opened my eyes.

I am truly grateful that I was hooked up to life support for 14 days. I am also grateful the doctors chose to give me Morphine and Demerol to allow my body to heal.

My parents wanted to let everyone know as fast as they could. I really have no idea how they made it happen but somehow, someone got the message to the rodeo announcer at the Canadian Finals Rodeo that I had woken up. He announced it as my friend Nikki was completing her round of barrel racing that night. Now taking a step back for a moment, please allow me to remind you we were a Rodeo family, so many of the people there who knew me would be at that event.

As I look through the book of notes, I see the one my mom wrote from that night too. Daphne, You have made me so happy. I love you so very much and you look so beautiful to me now today. Your smile was the best thing that has ever happened to me! I love you so very much. Rest tonight and we will talk tomorrow.

With all my love, Mom

I think one of the best notes was written by one of my friends the next day.

Hadley announced at the rodeo after Nikki's run that you opened your eyes and smiled. Well, there we were, me, Shauna, Mom, and Bev bawling our eyes out all through the bull riding. Just think 15000 people were cheering for you there last night. Yeah, we looked really cool.

So, we jumped around like fools for a while and I spent a lot of time walking up to strangers, hugging them, and saying "Daph opened her eyes!" (What a line, eh?) Everyone is really happy and I know it won't be long until you're back on Echo leaving a vapor trail. I love you and I'm so proud of you! Trish

Today, I am thankful my parents had a photographer come in to take pictures of me while I was still on life support and in my coma. I love seeing all of the different machines I was hooked up to. I share them as a badge of honor to anyone who wants to see exactly how far I have come. What I'm even more grateful for is how they had me on my good side and that the tube that was sticking out of my head to drain the fluid off, wasn't showing.

Once I was out of my coma, the process began of getting me more mobile. My healing journey was long, tedious, and painful.

The nurses propped me up into a sitting position and began to work on my mobility which had been limited from not moving for eighteen days. To this day, I still have issues with lying on a flatbed.

Sleeping flat on my back brings back deep-seated subconscious memories of the intense rage I felt of being in pain but not able to move or communicate. I am appalled how the anger and frustration still have a grip, at some points, in my life to this day. I am grateful though as I continue to learn skills and strategies to move past this frustration.

I was still on a feeding tube after I came out of my coma, I hated the tube and pulled it out several times. Thank God I only remember them putting it back in once. I gagged when the tube tickled the back of my throat because all I wanted to do was communicate. Growing up, my nickname was "Motor Mouth", and not being able to express myself left me frustrated and angry.

Initially, the nurses gave me a board to spell out words. My cognitive abilities were coming back but my body was not able to do what my brain was able to remember I could do. I was not the greatest speller at the best of times, so again, anger and frustration came in due to the fact people could not understand what I was trying to communicate. In fact, at one point, I even took the board and threw it across the room; I was so furious.

My parents finally figured out a simple way to communicate with me. I would lift one finger to say yes and two fingers to say no. Everyone got really good at asking me yes / no questions and my frustrations levels, at lacking communication, began to diminish.

When my throat finally healed enough for me to talk, I was left feeling intense burning pain. Once I could finally process what I wanted to say in my head, the words would not always come out the way I was wanting to say them. I spoke very softly and extremely slow. I could only imagine how difficult it must have been for everyone to listen to me try to get a thought out. I had been at the Royal Alexander hospital for almost two months when the doctors made the decision that I was ready to be transferred to the Glenrose Hospital to go through the rest of my rehabilitation.

I'm not going to sugarcoat it and say it was easy. The ups and downs taught me how to take everything one step at a time and know if I persevere, I can accomplish anything. I am grateful I made the choice to work through all the stages of my recovery and not stay stuck in a space of hopelessness.

I was very angry on my first day at the Glenrose hospital because my bed was on the floor and it had walls around it. Growing up in a rodeo family, I was pissed off at the mental image that they had me in a barn-box stall bed on the floor. It took time for me to make sense of why I was on the floor. I have since found out that brain injury patients thrash around in their sleep and they didn't want me to fall out of bed and injure myself more. I laugh now when I look back at the picture from that date and see the silly face I was making because I was so mad and indignant.

Yes, I dealt with a lot of intense anger and frustration because I was not able to do what I wanted to when I wanted to do it. Imagine not being able to get up and go to the bathroom whenever you wanted or just go outside for a walk. It was a daily struggle to stay determined to heal and not let the hopeless feelings take control. Learning to use anger and frustration as motivation was a process that was not easy for me to make.

The first time I looked into a mirror at myself, I realized that only one eye was fully open. My left eyelid was barely open and my pupil was turned out to the left side of my head. I remember how ashamed I was of how I looked, but at the same time, I was reminding myself of how grateful I should be that I was still alive. It was beginning to make sense why I was seeing double.

There was a lot of neurological damage caused when my head was smashed on the highway. My left eye did eventually work its way back to the center point and I have since had surgery to bring it back even more, but to this day, when I look up my left eye turns in.

I have also learned the fine art of not doing selfies while holding the camera up above my head so I do not look cross-eyed.

When I get tired the double vision comes back and reading is difficult, but I have learned ways around my challenges. Audible is a wonderful tool, I can listen to books whenever I want.

What strategies do you use to make your life easier?

CHAPTER 7 One Step At A Time

While I was at the Glenrose Rehabilitation Hospital I learned many lessons. Not only did all of the therapies help me to learn how to walk, talk, and take care of myself but they allowed me to see the world from a different perspective. These are lessons I am grateful for to this day.

I did not realize how much I had changed as an individual. I was no longer the young fifteen-year-old girl who could be active and out doing things. It was a huge realization, I had been given a second chance and a new beginning. I needed to choose wisely what I would do moving forward. I had to always make a plan before I did anything. It really was a pain in my butt but it worked for me, so I did what I had to do.

One day my parents were visiting me and I was complaining about how my feet hurt and my dad told me a short story that still sticks with me to this day. He said to me, "Daphne I used to complain that my feet hurt until the day I saw a man that had no feet." At that moment it really put everything into perspective. I realized how lucky I was to be alive and I just needed to figure out how to do things differently moving forward.

Being at the Glenrose for as long as I was, I saw many different kids come through Station 201. Another one of the many valuable gifts I learned was compassion. When I was feeling sorry for myself all I needed to do was look around the room and realize I did not have it so bad. I did not have pins drilled into my head to hold a broken neck in place and even though I was learning to write again, at least I still had my hand.

I learned that life is all about choice in how we see things. Even though things look to be at their worst, it is up to us how we choose to view them. It was very eye-opening to me how fast people were to judge how a situation may appear.

I was delighted to have the ability to go down to the cafeteria independently and yet I felt people were still looking at me like I was some sort of freak, judging me for my disabilities instead of looking at my accomplishments.

I had a dear friend gift me a poem on a little wallet card, I still have it on my nightstand table as a reminder. Whenever I am feeling down and like I can't make it through, I read this poem and it lifts my spirits and gives me strength and determination to keep moving forward.

Don't Quit
When things go wrong, as they sometimes will,
When the road you're trudging seems all uphill,
When the funds are low and the debts are high,
And you want to smile but you have to sigh,
When care is pressing you down a bit -
Rest if you must, but don't you quit.

Life is queer with its twists and turns.
As every one of us sometimes learns.
And many a fellow turns about when he
Might have won had he stuck it out.
Don't give up though the pace seems slow
You may succeed with another blow.

Often the goal is nearer than it seems
To a faint and faltering man;
Often the struggler has given up when he
Might have captured the victor's cup;
And he learned too late when the night came down,
How close he was to the golden crown.

Success is failure turned inside out -
The silver tint of the clouds of doubt,
And when you never can tell how close you are,
It may be near when it seems afar;
So stick to the fight when you're hardest hit -
It's when things seem worst, you must not quit.

When in your life did you keep on going when you felt like you wanted to quit?

Without realizing it at the time, I was inadvertently learning adaptability skills that would become the foundation for the rest of my life. Learning and growing one step at a time. I learned tolerance and patience from the many hours of repetitive, tedious therapies, knowing that healing takes time.

Little did I know how wonderful this gift would be. I learned that with my ability to move forward and keep going, I could accomplish anything. The numerous hours of different therapies I did to regain the muscles that had atrophied after many days of non-use were totally worth it. It used to drive me crazy that I would have to sit on the hard physiotherapy table and do leg lifts over and over, but I am grateful Cam made me do them because I can walk today. I did not understand how hard it would be to balance on a trampoline with no equilibrium.

The toughest one that I had to do was balance myself on a round board that was on a half-circle. My mom still has no idea how I did it. Neither do I to be completely honest. I just did what I had to do to get the heck out of there.

I remember the first time I stood up independently. I looked like a baby deer getting my feet under me for the first time. It was a very slow process and I was very shaky, but I followed all of the steps that Cam and I had been practicing for a few weeks. My mom was there to see it and I remember her standing there with her arms open wide like she was holding me up with an energetic bubble. I DID IT!

The Glenrose would allow therapy dogs on Station 201 for the kids but my parents made a plan to bring my barrel racing horse, Echo, to the hospital. Of course, they were not allowed to bring her in, but I was allowed to go outside, and seeing her fueled my desire to do whatever I had to do to get out of the hospital so I could see her every day.

We had the moment recorded on an old VHS videotape at one point but I am not sure where that has gotten to. She stood so quiet with me as I was outside.

Determination was the other skill that I honed in on. I may not have been able to do things the same way I was used to doing them, but I did not stop until I found a new way. I did not realize at the time how amazing this experience would be for me. Simply because I could not get them done the way I used to, did not mean it was not going to happen; it meant I needed to step out of the proverbial box and try a different way. This is a skill I now use every day.

What do you do differently than anyone else?

CHAPTER 8 Synchronicity

Some would say I was pig-headed and stubborn while working my way through my therapies. I choose instead, to use the words tenacious, dedicated, and persistent. At sixteen years old, I had no idea what I was going to do or how I was going to make it once I was out of the hospital, but one step at a time I knew I would make my way back.

It was not until after my eight-month stay between the two hospitals that I realized that my sense of hearing was heightened due to my other senses being decreased from the head injury. I would find noises deafening and it was really difficult for me to deal with, especially when I went back to school. Even just a tiny noise of someone tapping a pen on a desk would distract me, this now created a new challenge for me when I went back to high school the summer after getting out of the hospital.

I am grateful that the school made adaptations to help me be successful. They allowed a friend to write on carbon paper so that I could get notes from class and I could then just pay attention to what the teacher was saying. For exams, the teachers would provide me time in an office room with the door shut so that I would not be distracted by all of the different sounds, and gave me extra time to write my exams as my processing time was not as fast as others either. It was a blessing in itself. I was given extra time! The people at the school rallied around me to ensure that I had the opportunity to finish and graduate from high school. Now was the time to prove to myself the lessons I learned the past years could carry me forward.

I felt loved and had a new appreciation for others in high school. People accepted me for who I was now and were happy to see me back, even though I was not the same Daphne that they used to know. I looked different and I was not as quick-witted as I used to be, but my friends made me feel so welcomed.

I found that writing poetry was a way for me to express the many emotions I was working through. My favorite poem is…..

Roots

When you see a beautiful tree out in nature, you may not see the tangle of roots that lie beneath the surface.

Although the root may twist and turn, they have provided the tree with what it needs to grow.

Such is life.

There may be many twists and turns along the way, but that's what we draw our best experiences from. When life gets difficult take a deep breath and know that everything will work itself out.

It always does.

Daphne Dietrich

This poem is a great reminder to me that we all go through many things in our lives and we all have stories to share to help each other grow. Know that we are never alone. I learned that when I treat others the way I would like to be treated, life works out fairly well for me.

I acknowledge those who share their stories with me and am grateful every day for this amazing experience. No matter what, we will always make it through. The next chapter of my life proves this fact. It still amazes me how the perfect experiences come at the perfect moments even though we may not realize it at the time.

What unexpected gifts has the Universe brought into your world?

CHAPTER 9 Real World

After high school, I moved away from Calahoo to start working in the "real world." My roommate was going through some very difficult times and checked herself into the hospital so she could take care of her health. There I was all by myself, living in another town, working in jobs I really did not like, and trying to figure out what the hell to do next.

I was a waitress in two different restaurants and holy cow, what a rude awakening to the unrealistic expectations some employers have. It really did shock me how rude and inconsiderate some people could be. I truly have ultimate respect for waiters and waitresses in restaurants now that I never had before working in a restaurant.

I also worked at a job that made scratch-and-win tickets. I never even realized it was a thing but I guess they got to be made somewhere, right? It was long hours sitting at the end of a machine as the tickets rolled through. If something got cut, everything would shut down and we would have to find the pieces of the tickets to put with it. It was really crazy doing 12-hour shifts for very little pay, but I did what I had to do to make ends meet. It was very hard on the body doing the 12 hours in rotation.

How many times in your life have you worked at jobs that really sucked before you stood up for yourself to find something better?

I knew I needed something else but I was still fumbling around trying to figure out my way in the world. It really is amazing how the Universe is always listening. I realize now, that I always get what I ask for, whether I want it or not because that is when the rehabilitation practitioner program basically fell into my lap.

What better job could there be for me than a rehabilitation practitioner? I thought I am a person with a disability, I can help others learn new skills so that they can live independent lives too.

I was dealing with so much pain still and headaches that it was making my life almost debilitating. I was blessed to find an amazing chiropractor in another town an hour and a half away from me. I really didn't like the treatment styles of the ones in Barrhead. Dr. Yarrow was worth the drive. She was amazing at what she did and with her craniosacral treatments, my headaches began to decrease.

Craniosacral treatments are a form of bodywork or alternative therapy which uses gentle touch to palpate the synarthrodial joints of the cranium. It is based on fundamental misconceptions about the physiology of the human skull and is promoted as a cure-all for a variety of health conditions. It truly did wonders for me.

I was sad to find out that she was selling her practice but I am grateful that she sold it to the man who is still my chiropractor to this day, over 20 years later. Dr.Wandler is amazing at what he does and my life would not be what it is today without him. I am also honored to be one of his part-time laser technicians in his chiropractic office now. Opportunities are all around us when we are open to them.

When in your life have you been presented with an unexpected opportunity?

CHAPTER 10 Sharing The Light

I met Doug, who is now my husband, back in the late '90s. Neither of us knew it at the time, but as I reflect on it, we came together at the Smoky Lake rodeo. The same place where Dusty passed a few years before.

Doug was a truck driver at the time and I would only see him periodically when he was in town. It really was an awesome way to build a friendship first as we would simply go out and spend our time doing things we enjoyed doing, such as dancing, playing billiards, or going to concerts. We enjoyed spending time together and having fun. I really did not want to make any long-term commitments to anything or anyone as I focused my energy on schooling.

Getting through college was not a walk in the park. What would take my classmates two hours to complete an assignment would always take me at least double, if not triple the time. The college was very accommodating in assisting me. They provided carbon paper for me to share with a classmate, so when they took notes I could have a copy of them to go back over after class.

This, once again, allowed me to be able to listen to the professors and not be distracted. There was also an accommodation made for me to write my exams in a private room as well. My sense of hearing was still so acute that somebody tapping a pen on a desk would distract me and take me off my thought process.

Remember the horse Buck that I bought for a dollar when I was little? After owning him for many years, we sold him to a friend for a few years and when the friend wanted to sell him we bought him back. We sold him one more time to a family that was needing a reliable horse to teach their kids how to ride. A few years later that person wanted to sell him too.

It was then that he came down with colic. Colic in horses is defined as abdominal pain, but it is a clinical symptom rather than a diagnosis. The term colic can encompass all forms of gastrointestinal conditions which cause pain as well as other causes of abdominal pain not involving the gastrointestinal tract.

I was at work and my brother was very young when he saw Buck laying on the ground thrashing and rolling trying to get his belly to stop hurting. To this day, I still do not know how he instinctively knew to go put a halter on him and walk him around to ease the pain. His owner at the time decided to opt-out of getting the surgery done as there wasn't a guarantee that it would work. So for a week straight someone would go out to the barn to make sure that he walked around ovory hour on the hour to see if we could help him to get his twisted guts to unravel.

It really was heartbreaking to watch him wither away. He lasted until the Friday morning that my brother went out to say goodbye to him before school. Not ten minutes after he left Buck passed onto the other side. We now had a big, dead horse that wasn't even ours to deal with that we had to do something about. Again, the community came together in a small town. We had friends who owned a backhoe company from town. One of them came out at no charge and dug a hole on the hill where Buck used to like to stand so he could watch over all of the other horses. Thanks to our community coming together he was able to rest on the hill.

It really amazes me how people come together in a time of need and it still baffles me why we are not always like this.

When I graduated from the Rehabilitation Practitioner Program, I was blessed to support numerous individuals (from babies to seniors) learn many things, and gain their own independence.

It was very rewarding that I could be the one to help others along their own healing journeys.

I remember my first job outside of my practicum from school was working in a group home with four individuals who had multiple and varying disabilities. It was really wonderful helping them gain skills to live in their homes, like learning how to do their laundry and cook meals with little or no supervision. They

were long 12-hour shifts, but it worked well on Saturday and Sunday.

I had an amazing co-worker and we would create great adventures for us to all get out of the house and go to different places. I remember one time we were planning on going to this fabulous beach to have a picnic but I did not have a map. We thought we were following the proper signs but we ended up completely lost. It was so funny. Interestingly enough, for a wedding gift, she bought me an Alberta map. I still have the paper version of that in my vehicle 20 years later.

What one small thing have you done for someone else to brighten their day?

CHAPTER 11 Choices

It really is interesting how when we make the choice to change things in our life we get presented with different opportunities.

Doug and I had been married just over six months and we conceived a baby. I now needed to reconsider where I was working. I was still at the group home but I had cut back my hours. I had also started working in the city with a work opportunity program serving people with disabilities.

I was coming on about being seven months pregnant and Doug's grandmother passed away. My pregnancy was going fine, or so I thought, until I had our son three days after his grandma's funeral. We were visiting his sister's place when I hemorrhaged and Doug rushed me to the hospital. I was really scared. I had no idea what was going on or why I was bleeding as I was only seven months pregnant and I should not be having our baby yet.

I went up to the maternity ward and explained to them this is what's going on and they immediately got me onto a hospital bed and hooked me up to machines. I saw Doug come off the elevator looking for me and then I remember hearing the doctor say, "We're losing his heart rate." They rushed me out of the room, put the mask on my face and I do not remember anything after that. The doctor said he came nine weeks early.

They wouldn't allow Doug in the room when they gave me the crash C-section and I can only imagine the fear that he felt. I found out later that he had called my dad to let him know what was going on and my dad said she'll be fine, just call me back and let me know what she had.

I am pretty sure it shocked the heck out of him, but again my dad knew I would be okay. I was sad and scared. Our son was born nine weeks early and only weighed three pounds and four ounces.

We named him Koltin. He was in one hospital for just over a week and then they wanted to transfer him to another hospital. I told them that they could not do that because I was still a patient myself.

We had to coordinate my release from the hospital with his transfer to a different hospital so that he could be monitored and grow. He was only in that hospital for just over four more weeks. Koltin passed all of the tests and so they let him leave the hospital. He wasn't even 5 pounds yet.

My mom went and bought a baby doll from the store. We took the outfit off the doll and put it on him so that he had something to go home in. Talk about being scared and not sleeping because I wanted to make sure that he was breathing. The consequences of having Koltin brought into the world so quickly and unexpectedly, my milk did not have a chance to process so I had to take pills to get it flowing. Koltin never did breastfeed from me, so I rented an electric machine from the grocery store and pumped my milk every time he ate.

Again, I knew I needed to do this for him because he was so early he needed my milk to help his body grow strong. I did this faithfully every time he ate for six months. I had an abundance of breast milk in the freezer so he got my milk for the first year of his life.

I still chuckle when I think about the first interview that I had when I started looking at going back to work. I remember clear-as-day, they asked me the question "Have you been paying attention to the injury rates for the blue-collar workers from Red Deer North? I laughed and said, "No, I've been taking care of my premature baby." I think the interview was pretty much done after that. Needless to say, I never got called back for a second interview.

When in your life have you clearly been shown that something was not the right fit?

CHAPTER 12 True Healing

I was blessed to be hired to work for Work Opportunities. It was a program which supported individuals who had disabilities in the community at different jobs. I loved the diversity of it and I loved how they had a woodshop in the back too so that I could help clients build different items to sell to raise money for their organization.

After working in many different facets of this field for over eight years, I began to realize not everyone wanted to get better. I found it difficult to keep staying positive and I knew I needed to find something different. As rewarding as this job was, it was time for me to move on and find another one to help challenge me to learn and grow.

At the time, I was also still secretly dealing with a lot of pain both physically and emotionally. When the medications stopped working to dissipate my pain, I needed to look for other options that would work together to help me deal with my growing concerns.

I was blessed to go to a wedding and meet a beautiful acupuncturist who helped me dig deeper on my healing journey. I was terrified of needles, so it took me some mental convincing to go and see Dr. Sheryl Rist. She helped me so much over the years to deal with my pain, it has been a wonderful journey together.

I learned about the three C's of life.

Choices.

Chances.

Changes.

I learned that I must make a choice to take a chance, or my life would never change.

I knew I loved animals and I knew I liked helping, so I started looking for options of things I could do with helping animals.

Back to Google I went and the next adventure began.

I feel so blessed to have been able to follow my life path and experience these many different things. What I am most grateful for though, is how Doug has always stood beside me, even when I get off the wall ideas like wanting to do an online Animal Sciences Diploma. He never stands in my way and always picks me up when I fall down. I remember there were many nights that I would be beating myself up thinking I am never going to get through this and he would quietly walk up behind me to give me a loving squeeze. I was still working full-time so it took me about a year to get through that course, but I completed it and received my Animal Sciences diploma in 2006.

I have always been the sort of person who likes to try everything once. I was at the point in my life where I thought I had tried everything to get rid of my physical pain. Then one day, I remembered how my mom used to use magnets to heal injuries. She would use her hands to muscle test the best way to place a fridge magnet over the injured part of the body. Little did I know that this memory would ignite and inspire me to the new phase and unexpected journey of my life.

I love how the Universe synchronistically lined things up for me when I was ready.

I happened to be in the dollar store one day and saw torpedo style type magnets. I purchased the magnets and started carrying them in my pockets because someone mentioned to me it would help me feel better. I started carrying magnets every day. Little did I know how fast it would help.

I went to every dollar store in the city to purchase more magnets. I knew if it helped me feel better it would help others too.

At the time I had no clue why they helped. All I knew is that I felt better when I carried them, so that's what I did.

Anyone who knows me knows that if I do something, I do not do things just halfway.

I thank the Universe for guiding me to the many different resources that are available to find any information I was looking for!

Magnetite & Hematite

- Anti-inflammatory relieves muscle aches and pains, helps with asthma, blood, circulatory system, skin, and hair
- Hematite strengthens one's connection with the earth while grounding and protecting one's aura
- Brings courage, endurance, and vitality into one's life
- Enhances memory and original thought while stimulating focus and concentration
- Balances the body, mind, and spirit
- Dissolves negativity and prevents you from absorbing the negativity of others
- Boosts self-esteem and survivability, enhances willpower, reliability, and imparts confidence
- Helps to overcome addictions and compulsions or other forms of overindulgence like overeating and smoking
- Hematite regulates the blood supply by restoring and strengthening it.
- Hematite stimulates & supports the absorption of iron and regenerates tissue the formation of red blood cells for the kidneys
- Treats anxiety, insomnia, leg cramps, and aids spinal alignment and fractures
- Magnetite has powerful positive-negative polarities, sedating overactive organs and stimulating sluggish organs
- Aids meditation, visualization, and telepathy
- Alleviates fear, anger, and grief which provides stability by balancing the emotions with the intellect
- Balances trust and perspective in one's own intuition while attracting loyalty, commitment, and love
- Hematite provides recovery for the necessary healing energy

What I loved most about magnets is how they balanced the polarities of my body. They stimulated my underactive organs and sedated my overactive ones. I did not realize it at the time but the Universe was giving me the gentle nudges to dig deeper. That was when I found The Healing with Crystal Diploma course.

Little did I know the can of worms I was opening when I said yes to this amazing course.

It was a wonderfully put-together course that helped me remember things I didn't realize I had forgotten.

Like my dear friend Cynthia says:

"Have you ever remembered something you didn't know you forgot?"

Cynthia Gauvreau: www.cynthia.services

CHAPTER 13 Crystal Love

I truly felt like I was reading notes I had written long ago. It was a two-year program I completed in six months. I finished the program and received my Diploma in 2008. There were so many amazing things I had the opportunity to tap into.

It was such a blessing to see how different physical conditions were tied to emotional concerns too. It really amazed me at the relation between the crystals and how they helped the body. I was so grateful for the information and can of worms that I opened.

Not only did I learn about many of the different types of crystals and what magical things they could assist my body with. I also learned how to choose, clear, charge, and program my crystals of choice. Just when I thought it couldn't get any better, this course taught me the subtle Anatomy of chakras and Auras too. I was blown away when I completed the Crystal Treatments aka Laying on of hands portion of the course. I could energetically take myself back to when I was a little girl when my grandmother was teaching me the same thing.

I lapped up the Crystal Book Reading Suggestions at the end of the manual. There was so much information out there in the world and I could not get enough. It was really cute, one of the local crystal store business owners would joke with me whenever I was in his store. I was there a lot. One day he even said he was going to build me a little shelter in the back so I wouldn't have to go home. I could just stay there.

The easiest way I found that I could share the information with others was to make a simple nine-question crystal quiz I used this as a teaser. It was a great way for me to find out if someone was interested or not. Please allow me to share these questions with you now to discover which crystals would be helpful to you.

Crystal Quiz

Discover what crystal has the energy you need right now?

Check the Yes or No box after each one.

Remember, your answers may vary every time you take the test.

		YES	NO
1	I struggle with letting go of old thoughts.		
2	I despise my body I'm too (fat, skinny, short, tall)		
3	I frequently find that other people's moods are contagious. If someone is sad I find myself feeling sad, too.		
4	I have dreams and goals, but I find it tough to get from where I am to where I want to be.		
5	I have anxiety attacks easily.		
6	I am hypersensitive.		
7	I have trouble meditating.		
8	I dwell on other people's opinions of me.		
9	No matter how hard I try, I do not keep to my diet (or break another addiction).		

Crystal Quiz Answers

Choose the stone, which has the properties to help you.

For energy: Carry the stones with you, either around your neck or in a little pouch. Make sure you do not carry it with loose change, as it will pick up and absorb all of the energies from the money either positive or negative.

For meditation: When practicing by yourself you can either set it in front of you or hold it in your hand. When practicing meditation in a group setting, place the crystal in the center of the group for collective consciousness.

For healing: Ask the stone for its energies and utilize them. Set the crystal on the part of the body where you need the extra energy. At the end of the process, the stone is probably depleted of much of its energy. Thank your crystal and then cleanse it. Remember, most stones will retain these negative energies until cleared.

1	I struggle with letting go of old thoughts.	Clear Quartz	Called the mirror of the soul, it helps us to see who we truly are, free of limiting ideas and beliefs. Master Healer of all Healers. Effective for all conditions
2	I despise my body. I'm to (fat, skinny, short, tall)	Smokey Quartz	It establishes the most gentle and loving connection with the body of all the grounding stones. Nervous system, alleviates swelling, releases tension, and helps with stress. Helps with headache
3	I frequently find that other people's moods are contagious. If someone is sad I find myself feeling sad, too.	Hematite	The most grounding stone. Assists in reflecting, rather than absorbing, the moods of others. Strengthens the heart. Aids muscular system.

4	I have dreams and goals, but I find it tough to get from where I am to where I want to be.	Clear Quartz	A pointed crystal has the most focused energy and is the most powerful crystal to program for goals. It draws many blessings into one's life. Harmonizes energies, enhances spiritual awareness, and intensifies the awakening process.
5	I have anxiety attacks easily.	Rhodochrosite	Assists with slow deep breathing, which relaxes the solar plexus and sends needed oxygen to the brain.
6	I am hypersensitive.	Hematite	Helps us to shield from being over affected by opinions and or feelings of others.
7	I have trouble meditating.	Kyanite Hematite	This stone assists with meditation allowing a person to calm and grounded. This stone assists to stabilize and keep a person calm.
8	I dwell on other people's opinions of me.	Rose Quartz	When we nurture ourselves with self-love other people's opinions of us will usually mirror our own.
9	No matter how hard I try, I do not keep to my diet (or break another addiction).	Amethyst	Many people have used this stone to help in releasing addictions.

Disclaimer: I must share the standard disclaimer that I am not a doctor and cannot give out medical advice. Crystals for healing should be used as a complement to other therapies and not as a replacement for regular medical care.

After living in pain for more than 20 years, I was so grateful the Universe brought me crystals to help me on my journey to better health. It was magical to go with the flow of what assisted me to feel safe and comfortable in my own body.

Different groups and opportunities were presenting themselves to me to experience. For years, I had learned to say no to keep myself safe but I knew it was time to keep moving forward, and if I wanted things in my life to change I would need to make some more choices to lift me higher.

What is your go-to thing In life that brings you comfort and healing?

CHAPTER 14 Options

After completing the Healing With Crystal Diploma, I knew that it was time for me to leave the rehabilitation field but I had no idea what I wanted to do. I had my Rehabilitation Practitioner, Animal Science, and Healing with Crystals Diplomas, but no idea what the heck I wanted to do.

There were many days I would sit crying and wondering what my next step was going to be. To be honest, I felt so lost and was feeling like a failure. I read so many self-help books and watched so many different programs, I was making myself crazy. But, I went with the philosophy that I needed to try as many things as I could, and then I would be able to figure out what I wanted to do.

How many times in your life have you ever experienced this feeling? I was asking the Universe for a sign. Anything that might give me a clue as to what I should do. Randomly, one day I saw a post on Facebook that said "You only fail if you stop trying" and "I am not a product of my circumstances. I am a product of my decisions" Steven Covey ~ **n.a.**

So, I made the choice to do something about my situation.

I would go online every day and see if there were new jobs posted. There always was, but there was nothing that I was qualified for or I was overqualified for something, so it made finding a new job very difficult.

I would go for walks, I would drive to different places using different routes just to try new things and open up my mind to new opportunities.

That was when I started my gratitude list of the things that I was grateful for in my life. It was really interesting how when I consistently did write down what I was grateful for, the Universe would always bring more to my life to celebrate and be grateful for.

Randomly, an opportunity to work in a bank came along. I felt that it would be a new challenge and my next journey. Yes, I am aware it makes no sense at all, but my heart and mind wanted me to do something different and I was always up for a challenge. Looking back now I realize it was not random at all, it was exactly what I needed to at the time.

It was very, very challenging for sure. Two weeks of intensive banking boot camp was a lot for my brain to take in, but I did the best I could at the time. I made friends with one of the other new girls and we worked together to learn the massive load of Information. In my five-year banking career, there were many times when I wanted to walk away. I am grateful I chose to stay. I learned many things and grew deeply as an individual.

I was blessed to hold many different roles while working in the bank. I started off as a customer service representative, which in some ways was great because there were systems in place in which I needed to follow, but it was difficult because there were so many steps to everything. I loved that role though because it allowed me to visit with different people all day every day. It worked very well with my "motor mouth" from childhood.

I will always be forever grateful to D'Arcy, the manager at the branch where I was working, who saw my potential and allowed me to be the being that I was. When I was working as a coordinator in the beginning it was difficult. It was all new systems and all-new ways of doing things. He explained it to me in a wonderful way, how it was kind of like getting ready for a dinner party.

You know how you need to prep and cook the vegetables while the meat is cooking in the oven and you need to be getting the salad ready as well? That's kind of how the coordinator role worked too. I needed to be answering phones, dealing with emails, booking appointments, and getting clients into the appropriate offices, all while I was greeting everybody that was going in and out of the building.

It was really a wonderful role for me because I did not have to sit in one spot and I got to see absolutely everybody that came in and out of the bank.

A dear friend of mine shared a Neuro-Linguistic programming course with me. I got to go and be a part of this course for the entire weekend. I felt that it would help me in my role at the bank to learn how to better communicate with people. However, I was mistaken, the instructor brought me to tears trying to coach me through releasing and letting go of the memory of Dusty instead.

She did not believe in Spirit guides and she felt I needed to release and let him go. Even though at the time, I knew I needed his assistance as one of my guides, she pushed what she felt was right. You know how there is crying and then there is ugly crying. Well, I was ugly crying for sure.

This was an amazing lesson that really helped me see so many things from a different perspective. Since I have been able to do and try as many things as I have, I am grateful to see that we are all doing the best we can at the time. When we know better, then we do better.

Everyone is unique and just because one thing works for someone else does not mean that it has to work for you too. We get to make the choice of what we do each and every day. I learned for myself, firsthand, that I am "Not" a follower. I do what I need to do for myself and my family with the utmost love and compassion.

When did you step into choosing you first?

CHAPTER 15 Opportunities Are All Around Us

Some like to call me a trendsetter or a trailblazer. If I had not listened to my intuition I would not be where I am today. I love how life synchronistically brings things to me when I am ready.

I was working in the bank and was a "secret rock carrier." This was back before it was cool to carry crystals. There were only a few people at the bank that knew I was packing "rocks."

One day, D'Arcy had just returned from vacationing in Phoenix. He brought me back a pair of magnet earrings. D'Arcy made a joke about how the magnets would balance my brain. I laughed at his comment because I am not sure if he really realized how right he really was. He thought I might find them helpful in my life, and as it turns out, I think it was probably the most life-changing thing anyone could have done for me.

Let me take a step back for a moment, D'Arcy knew I had come back from a brain injury and he also knew how much I loved magnets. I share this to let you know he also had a daughter that survived a massive head injury and I was always grateful for his knowledge and humor. Even though he would probably never admit it, there was an unspoken understanding that if I ever needed help at work I could go to him.

The magnet earrings lit a small spark in me and grew from there. I am forever grateful for how D'Arcy saw the light in me and fanned my flames of creativity to reach for more.

I loved how I felt when I wore them and I wanted more pairs of magnet earrings, but because they were brought in from the states I could not find them in Edmonton. I wanted more pairs for myself, so I made the choice to start making my own.

I had no idea what I was doing but with trial and error 101, I got it figured out. It wasn't until I had over 40 pairs of earrings that my loving and supportive husband said to me, "Honey, I think you should show these to some of your friends. They might like to buy them too."

Daphne's Healing Hands was birthed the day I made the choice to share what I had created. Many suggested that maybe I should start making necklaces and bracelets to go with these fabulous earrings and, even though I had no idea what I was doing, I tapped into my intuition and followed my gut.

The opportunities presented themselves to me to go to different markets and venues to sell my creations and I went with it, following what I was guided to do. It brought my heart such joy to be making these one-of-a-kind healing crystal creations for my friends and family.

Like I said before, I love how the Universe brings inspiration and opportunities into my life when I'm ready for them. I was working at a new location at the bank and this magical lady came in carrying this contraption on her shoulder that was "lighting up." Long story short, the magical light turned out to be a cold laser with healing light coming out of it. Little did I know how this would send me into the next chapter on my healing journey.

How open are you to seeing opportunities when they present themselves?

CHAPTER 16 I Am…….

It was awesome that I was given the opportunity to train with the man who created the laser when he was in town over a two-year period. I felt so blessed I was able to get a binder of information together to share with others. I then found out a lady who was training with me also had these really cool sacred geometry energy tools which I added to my toolbox of complementary healing modalities.

While working at the bank one day, one of my customers, a trainer of horses at the local racetrack, asked me if I could come and help her injured horse. I knew what the laser could do and that it would help, so I accepted her request.

It was wonderful being back and spending time with the horses since I was no longer able to ride. The horse won its first race after receiving only four treatments. The injury never came back either, which lit my heart on fire and sent me looking for more people and animals to help.

It was around that time I was getting busier with markets and only working part-time at the bank. I asked the Universe if this is what I'm supposed to be doing, please make me busy enough that I don't need to work at the bank anymore. Magically appointments started coming in and more people were ordering custom pieces of crystal healing creations for themselves and their animals.

This was also around the time I started to dabble with Manifesting things. I would ask for certain things or events to present themselves in my life and it would blow my mind how they always showed up.

I also learned to be careful what I would ask for because the Universe would bring it to me. I'm not going to lie, I kind of wish I would have learned this lesson sooner. It's okay though. I truly believe that each and every one of us has lessons to learn in this lifetime.

Had I not chased what I thought were my dreams, I would not have realized what I was really needing and wanting were right in front of me. My life would have turned out very differently.

I remember at one point I even took the time to write down in red pen many positive affirmations and voice record them so I could listen to them daily. Please know that I am not recommending you do the same as me unless you are really drawn to it. I am simply sharing these here so that if some stand out for you, you can write them down too.

- I am so happy and grateful, I Am accepting who I am now in this moment. I forgive myself for not seeing the gifts that I Am Love, unconditional love that knows no judgments. Thankfulness for the awareness and the opportunity to choose differently. To show up as I am and know that I Am Worthy and I Am Enough.

- I am so happy and grateful the Universe is aligning me with people, things, and situations that match the energy I am putting out. The more I improve myself and raise my vibration the more I will see the things that are magical and beneficial to my well-being.

- I welcome a new path, new energy, new connections, new experiences, new thoughts, and new ideas. I am open to all things new, different, and adventurous. I am ready for new beginnings.

- My peace begins with me and when I allow my true self to flourish I feel wonderful and alive.

- I wake with energy and optimism because I'm connected to the Universe.

- I inhale confidence and exhale fear.

- I am so happy and grateful for the new beginnings that are surrounding me in my life.

- I am getting inspired and letting go of what no longer serves my highest good.

- I am so happy and grateful my success story is happening and it is inspiring others to be, do, and have whatever it is they want in their lives.

- What is destined for me to be will never pass me by. I'm giving hope to so many people.

- I am so happy and grateful for the first of unexpected positive changes that are happening in my life and finances.

- I am so happy and grateful to be receiving the miracles and elevating my quality of life.

- I am so grateful and happy the Universe is bringing clients to me who are ready to receive my assistance, purchase my services, and order my custom creations.

- I am attracting people who are helping me with my purpose and reach for more.

- All is well and getting better in my life every day.

- I am at peace with my past.

- I am welcoming this new transformation.

- I am welcoming growth.

- I am welcoming in abundance.

- I am aware of what I need.

- I am ready for the true abundance that is coming into my life in both seen and unseen ways.

- The abundance I seek in whatever form starts within me.

- I will never doubt.

- My faith and trust produced miracles in my life.

- I am ready to create my dreams.

- I am worthy and whole.

- I am courageous and speak my truth.

- I have integrity and my friends trust me.

- I am a powerful creator.

- The Universe always provides for me everything that I need and want.

- I am gifted and able.

- I am fruitful and generous.

- I intend to chill the F out and ask the Universe for guidance.

- I'm experiencing breakthroughs, blessings, and abundance.

- I am so happy and grateful that when people spend enough time with me they realize that everything is going to be okay.

- I'm so happy that I can share my gifts to help others to calm their souls while opening their minds to heal their bodies from the inside out.

- Divine timing is always on my side and the Universe is conspiring in my favour. Prosperity flows through me at all times.

- I am so grateful that when I am meeting and connecting with people, they bring out the best in me and remind me that I am worth it.

- I'm surrounding myself with people who make me feel hungry for life, touch my heart, and nourish my soul.

- I am safe, I am loved, and I am protected.

- I'm open to the many wonderful and unexpected opportunities the Universe is presenting me.
- I am so grateful for a clear life path that has less confusion, good ideas, miracles, spiritual inspirations, positive motivators, and money flooding in all around me.
- I am standing in my power and speaking my truth.
- Determination and dedication equal success.
- I am so happy and grateful for the positive energy that is flying into my life at this time and the miracles I am living.
- I am so happy and grateful to be manifesting new clients every day.
- I am welcoming the exciting adventures as the financial abundance flows into my life with ease and grace.
- I am so happy and grateful that I'm now living up to my potential and listening to my voice from within.
- I am smartening up. I am learning from everything and smartening up. The better and smarter I can do something, the more efficient I will be. I am always striving to find a better way and smartening up.
- There is power in me and I am strong.
- I am proud of who I am and I trust the person I have become.
- I am aware of the choices I make to control my life.
- I love and accept myself for who I am today.
- I am a humble and proud person who is beautiful on the inside and out.
- I am a blessed, creative, connected, and expressive person who is valued for what I do.
- I let go and allow the Universe to do its thing.
- I'm so happy and grateful to be entering this new age of expansion. I'm excited to know that what I focus on, I manifest with ease and grace.

- I'm so grateful and happy for the energetic and positive shift that is happening right now. I'm excited for the decluttering and clearing out of old energy. I am grateful for the communication breakthroughs and the true feelings to surface and unveil. I am so excited for healthier and deeper still connections that are building in my life to not only assist me with my emotional cleansing and healing but also increase the abundance and fortune coming into my life with ease and grace.

- Huge blessings are on their way from the Universe.

- I do the right thing even when no one is looking.

- I'm so happy and grateful and know that everything that is truly mine will come to me in Divine time.

- I am surrounding myself with people who are passionate. I need to be, do, and have more in my life.

- I'm so happy and grateful to be calling for the energy of abundance to support my dreams and desires.

I found all of these to be very helpful in my life at the time. I found that they really helped me focus on that which I chose to see in my world. I'm not saying that my world was one hundred percent perfect by any means, but when I went through this list every morning before I got out of bed and every night before I went to sleep, my perspectives shifted.

What are your I AM statements?

CHAPTER 17 Creative Workshop

To this day, one of my favourite inspirational websites I have found is the Abraham-Hicks Publications website.

There are so many amazing pieces that really helped me get out of my head and back into my heart. Please check out their site and find the piece that most resonates with you:

All of the material is by Abraham-Hicks, © by Jerry & Esther Hicks, the name of the publication from which the material used was excerpted, the AbrahamHicks.com website, and the contact phone number, (830) 755-2299

I find it so fascinating how there are so many different opportunities to experience new things when I am open to it.

My dear Friend Nancy has an amazing section in her Recover Your Joy Program called

Scripting Your Dream Day. With her permission, I am able to share pieces of it here with all of you. Setting a clear intention and focused desire, is a magical process to use for future events that you want to bring a positive vibration into.

Scripting is a law of attraction technique that she found, that is offered by Abraham-Hicks in her book "Ask and It Is Given" 2004 Hay House Inc., where you write a story about your life as you want it to be. Nancy tells us you can use the scripting process if you want to:

- Deliberately create your experiences.
- Get more specific about your desires.
- Have the thrill of writing what you would like to experience and then seeing how the Universe delivers what you described.
- Consciously experience the power of your focused thoughts.
- Create your day in advance (you can script every part of your day or just a segment of it).

She goes on to tell us that you can write about anything that you want: a relationship, your dream home, improved health, the perfect job, your ideal day, or winning the lottery. Anything goes – whatever you want to manifest and experience.

Nancy recommends starting by identifying yourself as the main character, then identifying other characters in the scenario, and then writing the plot of your story.

Nancy would like you to remember these additional tips when scripting:

- Write it as if it already happened.
- Include your emotions – how do you feel?
- Include all your senses – what do you see, hear, smell, touch?
- Keep it fun and positive – use words that make you feel good
- Keep it lighthearted
- Express appreciation, "I love that…," "I love feeling…"
- Read your script regularly

It is most effective if you write your script by hand because writing is your most powerful point of focus. Nancy reminds us that scripting assists you in telling the Universe the way you want it to be.

If there is something you want that has not yet manifested, it is a good way to speed it up.

It will help you break your habit of talking about things the way they are, and start talking about how you would like them to be. Scripting will help you shift your vibration deliberately to what you want. You are less likely to bring to your point of focus thoughts of doubt or disbelief. One final thought from Nancy is that scripting is an exercise in self-empowerment. She asks you to ponder what lies ahead for you, Nancy encourages you to create your own future rather than letting it happen to you. Be the empowered creator of your own story!

At one point, I was even blessed to go to an amazing event at the Telus World of Science here in Edmonton, Alberta Canada, with my dear friend Sandra. It was called "Mesmerica."

"MESMERICA 360 is a unique visual music journey designed to stimulate the mind and senses, bringing together the music of Grammy-nominated composer and percussionist James Hood together with visually-hypnotic, 3D animated art curated from artists around the world. Experience a stunning and immersive 360 fulldome projection with 5:1 surround sound in Planetariums and Dome Theaters across the US and Canada."

We laid on our backs in the centre of the room and watched beautiful colours as the music and lights danced around us for an hour and a half.

Throughout the presentation he spoke with such powerful words, it was beautiful.

"Why do we waste so much of our lives with this gift we have been given? Worrying about the future or dwelling on the past.

Whatever happened yesterday does not need to influence our future. We owe it to ourselves to expand our thinking, to live passionately, activate our minds to shamelessly fire our imaginations to make the most of our short time here on this Earth.

I want to wish you happiness, real long lasting happiness. This kind of happiness does not exist in another time, or at another place, or to another person.

It can happen in this place, and in this time, and to you.

I believe that happiness is our natural state. So, I hope you go from this place with a renewed vitality and gratitude for life. With a revitalized commitment to live a joyful and fulfilling life. However that may look to you and in this endeavour. Your mind can be a powerful eye, It makes everything possible.

So, be well, be happy, and be confident in your own power to create a wonderful life for yourself.

Full of beauty, laughter, friendship and connection.

You were birthed from something miraculous and I encourage you to see it fully in yourselves and all those around you.

I wish you love, luck and great joy on your journey. Thank you for attending."

Who I later found out was James Hood. I am so grateful that I said yes to attending this amazing event.

For me, it always brings me such a sense of peace when I hear this. It really helps me to put things back into perspective and remember what is important in my life.

As I grow older, I am beginning to truly understand my life. I am the most successful person I can be when I am doing what works for me. When I stopped chasing after someone else's dreams; opportunities began presenting themselves to me.

What are you doing for you today?

CHAPTER 18 Manifesting

I realize there are many ways to do many things. I am blessed with many friends who have numerous talents. My dear friend Alli MacKenzie taught me the power of Manifestation. With her permission, I am honored to share it with you here.

5 steps to Harness Magic and Manifest Results.
1. Be VERY clear and specific on what you want/need/desire. The Universe is ALWAYS listening! Yup, even when you're having your morning poop, singing along to your fav Lizzo song. She's always co-creating with you, and she always delivers. Instead of, "I want a new car!" Say, "I want to purchase a 2019 Tesla and sell my current car because it's on its last leg, and I really want to drive something that's better for the environment."
2. Envision your results. Use your imagination here! Visualize yourself experiencing the results you desire and do this often! Close your eyes and imagine yourself selling your car to someone who could really use the parts, see yourself driving out of the lot in your new Tesla; driving down the open road with Tom Cochrane cranked singing, "Life is a highway!" Or whatever you like to listen to.
3. Be open to other possibilities. Even though you have an amazing vision for yourself, perhaps the Universe has an even sweeter deal tucked up her sleeve? Remember, she's always co-creating with you for your highest good.
4. Practice patience. This is a toughy. Especially in our very modern-day world where tweets and toots are granted with the click of a button. We need to slow down a little bit. Enjoy the process and engage in some delayed gratification. When you plant a flower, do you dig it up every day to see how it's growing, or do you simply give it what it needs (water, sun, healthy soil, time) and let it be? Quit diggin' up your flowers!
5. TRUST THE PROCESS. Divine timing truly is divine. What you seek will come to you when it's meant to. Continue forward. Keep taking positive action steps toward your goals, your visions, and your dreams. They will come to Life when the time is right.

Keep Living and Loving, Dear One.

I love how her 5 step process is so crisp and concise.

Alli is such an exceptional woman! She posted something the other day that had some more "I Am" statements with it

"I Am supported by mother Earth and connected to the Universe.

I Am Divinely-Guided every step of my way.

Creating Alignment.

This is a mantra she uses daily too:

- Guide me when I'm feeling stuck
- Ground me when my head's in the clouds
- Connect me to the Universe when I feel lost

Words are so very powerful. They can create a positive, influential impact that forever changes the course of your Life.

Words CAN uplift you. Words can increase your energetic vibration. Words can help heal.

I invite you to experiment with this mantra today. Listen and feel into the shifts that take place within your body, mind, and soul.

How does it feel?

I am forever grateful for Alli MacKenzie in my life.

In a way, I kind of wished I would have learned these things a little bit sooner but, in reality, had I learned them sooner I may not have had the many wonderful experiences I have had. I love how we both are speaking the same overall message of language and process and how they are so different.

What is your favorite inspirational quote?

CHAPTER 19 Gratitude

I am so happy and grateful the Universe has supported me and blessed me with my purpose of being a wife, a mother, and a business owner. I am so honored to be an energy healing conduit for others. I also realize that I can not go back and change the past but I am able to dissolve my trapped energy and physical pain by letting the past be what it was. I recently saw a brief video that blew my mind.

It talked about when we release things we are actually ignoring them but when we let them be what they are, we are accepting all the lessons that we have learned through those experiences, good or bad.

I now see the world on a bigger and more colorful scale, and how I fit into it. I stopped beating myself up for what I could not change and had no control over. I now make the conscious choice to live in the present moment and make decisions that will lift me and the people in my life higher.

Please let me make it clear, it has not been all sunshine and roses getting to where I am today. There is always something to deal with and it has taken me over a decade to finally come to these realizations.

I practice gratitude daily with myself and others. After going through my morning ritual of stretching and saying thank you, I send my messages to friends sharing my daily gratitude list. It really is nice to see what my friends are grateful for too. It really helps me start my day off on a positive note.

What I realize now is my brain injury actually activated my brain so I could tap into a higher consciousness of being. I am noticing the patterns in my life as a gift instead of a problem. I am seeing how each and every person I encounter in life has been an integral part of my journey along the way.

Had I not volunteered to help a friend at her women's empowerment event, I would not have met Kim, who happened to be friends with Michelle. Michelle and I had developed a friendship and she then introduced me to Maxine and Mark.

Maxine and Mark were working on an amazing initiative called Big Hearts Tiny Houses. They took recycled pallets and turned them into tiny houses for people to live in. They both helped me to gain confidence in myself to do things I never thought about doing, like helping to build a shop for us to build the tiny houses in. I never thought I would be able to go up a ladder and paint the side of a house. Maxine would not let me say that I could not do something. I even remember one time she asked me to help her move a stack of pallets and I told her I couldn't. Maxine never took no for an answer. I am forever grateful for how she helped me push through some of my greatest fears only to realize that it really was not a big deal after all.

I am grateful how Mark reminded me that it was perfect for me to be who I am just the way I am. I felt so honored when he introduced me to Ginette Biro.

She reminded me that we are all unique and special people. I later found out that Ginette is divinely connected and an amazing soul. She is a powerful medium who is clairaudient, clairvoyant, clairsentient, and claircognizant. Ginette can hear, see, feel and know information from spirit and other dimensions.

Since she was a child, Ginette has been channeling beings from the 4th to 12th dimensions, connecting people to the other side and bringing messages to inspire and inform our world.

Ginette has many spirit guides and ascended masters and beings who are guiding her to support the planet in its ascension. In addition to these remarkable gifts, she has spent soul time on the other side through a near-death experience too. This allowed her to see and understand how our life blueprint and soul's journey actually work.

Ginette has crossed over and back and now has a unique insight to guide others on their life path. She is dedicated to using that knowledge to support people on their own journeys.

Prior to a career using her spiritual gifts, Ginette pursued science receiving a Bachelor of Kinesiology and a Diploma of Sports Medicine, and practiced as a kinesiologist. She is also a talented singer and musician, performing internationally for the Canadian Armed forces. After traveling to Afghanistan, Europe, North Pole, and the United Arab Emirates, Ginette received the Humanitarian of the Year Award in 2009 from the BC Country Music Awards for her work.

Charismatic, warm, and relatable, Ginette can take difficult esoteric topics and explain them in a way that's easy to understand. She has the ability to answer the questions that inspire, haunt, mesmerize and intrigue, and use her other-worldly access to expand insight into life here on earth. Ginette is entertaining and a magical storyteller and is destined to become one of the great female spiritual leaders of our time. I am honored to be able to call her my friend.

We each have our own reality and our own dimensions. Which is what creates the amazing uniqueness of the Universe as a whole and makes life so interesting. Ginette helped me to discover what really happened when I was in my coma here on the 3D plane.

Due to the trauma of my injuries, for many years, I have not even really thought about what happened while I was in my coma. I say that I chose to come back to share with and show people that, ya shit can happen, but when we make the choice to overcome any obstacle, we can.

Ginette, however, connected with my spirit guides and they let us know that this was the only way they could get me to slow down long enough for them to share with me what they need to share with my 15-year-old brain, to be able to carry it forward.

My guides told her the rainbow council bathed me in the rainbow colours, to assist me in unlearning any and all of the limiting beliefs which I had learned in my first fifteen years of life. They helped me to let go of all of the negativity I no longer needed, so

I could be my true self. This blew my mind when I first heard it too.

OK.

Stop.

Close your eyes and take a deep breath in and hold it at the top.

Then let it out slowly.

That sense of calm and release you feel is the exact feeling I had when I was on the other side.

No pain, no worries, no stress. Simply bliss.

I will do my best to try to and share what I felt.

Tune Into your Inner being and listen to whatever angelic frequency is playing in your head right now.

Picture yourself sitting in a claw foot bathtub with your knees up to your chest.

Now feel a warm blanket of warmth and rainbow colors rolling across your body in waves.

That beautiful feeling of calm, peace, love, and joy you are experiencing is what I felt.

My cellular DNA was being reprogrammed and the only way I can describe it in human terms is like seeing the computer programing screen of numbers and letters.

It has taken me many years to come to terms with this and be able to talk openly about it. There really are no earthy words to even begin to explain the complete oneness I felt when I was there.

It makes so much sense now though. Light is the purest form of energy. My healing happened through the light and different frequencies. The different rays and colors allowed the light to permeate the different parts of my body, mind, and spirit.

Just like my Aunt Gloria was tapped in here on this 3D plane. She was working on me here while the rainbow council was giving me the valuable information to come back here to share.

For me, it is more "like a knowing" of what I need to do in each moment. I ask, and Spirit responds. Please believe me when I say this was not an immediate thing for me when I woke up out of my coma. I needed to come back here and live. I needed to truly experience life and be grateful for the many experiences, even though I did not realize it at the time.

When people ask me how I do what I do. The only answer I can give is I get out of my own way and do what I am guided to do. Everything is energy and I am a conduit. What I do is several years ahead of where science is at and why I am so drawn to use the tools that I do. The cold laser light therapy tool provides photons to the cells of our body so they can heal and regenerate. It is still a very useful and futuristic modality that partners well with the crystals and sacred geometry tools that I use.

I share Unconditional Universal Love. When I am being the conduit for animals or people in person, I allow my hands to channel out any of the stuck energies and channel in the positive Universal life force energy. Energy knows no bounds and I feel so blessed that I am able to send distant energy work to animals and people around the world now.

There were many times I have asked Spirit about what I am to know and many times they told me "It's not yet time."

One day I was feeling rather frustrated with this process so I decided to sit down with my guides and have a talk. They like to come to me in interesting ways to share what they are wanting to tell me.

At first, I heard a line from the song Don't Worry Be Happy, Every little thing is going to be alright.

77

Then I heard All You Need is Love.

When I asked them what the heck I am supposed to share with others that they taught me while I was on the other side, they showed me a Big flashing sign of the word Love.

I am blessed to now realize that life is simple and it does not need to be complicated. I am grateful that there are more people waking up to being open to new opportunities to experience energy.

I am here to be and share Love.

In what areas of your life would you like to gain more understanding?

CHAPTER 20 Polarities

I am grateful for Ginette and her description of her experiences as a child in her book, "Avalon to Aurora - Lessons from the other side to guide your life on earth", published December 12, 2020. Her fevers were the way she was given her light code information. As I read her book it was like I could hear the angels singing and saying "Now you are ready."

Ginette explains Light Code information as the energy patterns and frequencies from the higher realms that can be activated for ascension in this world. For her, this light code information required her body to be heated in order to receive it and store it on a cellular level.

For me, I was on life support for 2 weeks and in a coma for 18 days. I am so blessed that Spirit brought Ginette and myself together when it did. It makes so much sense when she says in her book that her fevers opened the door for her soul to journey far and wide to gain visual understandings of consciousness on all levels of life - from atomic to cosmic - that would be available for her to make sense of when she was older. It became embedded and encoded light information waiting and ready to surface at the right time.

There was never any doubt that I would not be able to come back from my horrible car accident. When the doctors took me off life support and I came out of my coma, I knew I would do whatever it took to regain my life.

At the beginning of my healing Journey, I really had no idea what I was facing but I always knew that there was a way that I would figure it out. To this day, I still feel I can make it through any of life's challenges.

Yes, I am wired a little bit differently than everybody else and it is completely 1000% okay because I always get things done.

It might not be the way that you would like me to do it but I always figured out a way to make it happen.

I was asked to be a vendor at a psychic fair market and I had a lady come over to me who was dealing with a lot of pain from fibromyalgia. I asked her to stand on the sacred geometry rings as I used my triple pyramid to sweep through her energies to detach any hooks, cords, or energies that didn't need to be there anymore.

As I was working on her a crowd formed around me to see what was going on as they usually did when I am at these types of events. Hence the reason I would position the people I was assisting to face the back of my booth. I always want the people I am helping to be as relaxed as they can be.

There was one lady that was standing on the edge with her arms crossed looking at me with her brow furrowed. I saw this look and was a little bit taken back by it. When I was done being the conduit for the lady with fibromyalgia and she walked away with no pain the other lady walked over to me and said "Do you realize that you have a plethora of guides and angels that are surrounding you right now?" I smiled and nodded my head yes. She continued, "And do you realize that you're doing what they're telling you to do before they even tell you to do it?" I smiled again and asked her, "Isn't that the way everyone does it?."

It was then that I realized that what I am here to do is help others tap into their own intuitive abilities to be able to heal themselves in whatever way works for them. I think it is amazing how there are so many options available and it warms my heart when I can help others find what will help them too.

My motto became "Go with the flow"

What is your favorite "Go with the flow" thing to do?

CHAPTER 21 Inspiration

Compassionate sharing of what we know with others I feel is the only way we can move forward on this planet. We didn't come to this earth to remain separate and compete with each other. We came to this planet to come together in community. I know that I am a much happier person when I am sharing, growing, and learning with others.

Like my friend Denise Belka says, "If we understood how the Universe really worked our brains would explode."

What started as a hobby 10 years ago is now my full-time business of Daphne's Healing Hands. It really is wonderful when I get to be the conduit to channel energies. It is so much fun being able to facilitate balancing, restoring, and rejuvenating energies for both animals and people.

It was not until I tapped into my tribe of like-minded people that I was able to move forward and rise above the suffering that I was going through so that I could help others do the same. If someone would have told me years ago that this is where I would be today I know I would have laughed. I remember when I used to think that working forty hours a week for someone else was the best way to secure my future.

People look at me and say that I am a Healer. I chuckle and say, "Yes I am, because I healed myself."

We are all healers. A healer is not someone who heals you. A healer is someone who will hold space for you while you awaken your inner healer, so that you may heal yourself. When we all rise up we all share our light with others. First and foremost, we need to believe in ourselves to "Be the Being We Were Born To Be" so we can step into our greatness.

Anyone that knows me knows that I will never quit and when times get tough I do what I have to do to make it through. If I stumble, I get back up. What happened yesterday no longer matters. Today is another day, so I get back on track and move closer to my dreams and goals.

You can do it too.

One step at a time.

Moving forward and not stopping.

I saw a quote just the other day "Someone who drowns in 7 feet of water is just as dead as someone who drowns in 20 feet of water. Stop comparing traumas, stop belittling you or anyone else who has trouble because it wasn't 'as bad' as someone else's. This isn't a competition; we all deserve support and recovery." ~ Casey ~

Like Chris Close says

"A scar does not form on the dying, a scar means I survived"

I was reminded by a friend to accept and validate myself about how much I have Inspired others who crossed my path. I really do not think about it, but yes, I am "That Friend" who will always lift you higher and see the silver lining!

My magical friend Christina Marie shared a post one day that she wrote 6 years ago that inspired me.

Be, with the people that bring out the best in you.

Care about those who earn and prove their worthiness to be a part of your life.

Laugh with those you love and hold dear in your heart.

Say the words you mean as you never know if they could be the last.

Embrace each moment in the present making a memory forever etched in time.

Connect on a deeper level with those receptive, always speaking your truth.

Appreciate all the qualities in those around you as they are a mirrored reflection of yourself.

Love authentically and unconditionally always as it offers healing in this often hard world.

Remember, we are all interconnected as one.

And in the end, the best things in life are truly free.

Smiles from the inside outs.

This is a beautiful reminder for all of us to live each day to the fullest because the world is truly a magical place when we choose to see it that way.

I want to inspire people to look at me and say, "because of you I didn't give up!" I believe that I chose this path to share with others the true magic of life.

My many experiences are my driving force in helping others to see how they too can take the steps to heal their own bodies and find the sparkle in their eyes again. Honor the creator that you are and how that fits for you. When you can focus on what you want in your life it creates a ripple that permeates to others.

Another soul sister of mine helped me to see that I choose to move beyond my story and not stay stuck in it. I am blessed to have been published in the first two books of the Sacred Hearts Rising anthology series. I really never thought that anyone would want to hear my story because I didn't really see any value in it but when Brenda Hammon who was the publisher would not let me say no, I wrote the first chapter, "ROOTS."

I realize now it was written in a fairly synchronistic form with no emotion attached to it. Really, it did not surprise me as I told the story so many times that I really have no emotion to it. When I wrote the second chapter, "HOW I FOUND MY WINGS", I took a step back and looked a little deeper for what the next step was.

I was shocked when Brenda told me that I was going to be one of the speakers at the second annual book launch. Anybody who knows me knows that I have no problem speaking in front of people, but, oh my God, she wanted me to be on a stage and share something inspirational.

What would I say......

Where would I start.........

I was scared and did not know if I could do it, but then I realized she was handing me this opportunity I couldn't turn down. I took the steps necessary to figure out how to do a slideshow on my computer, I had never done that before.

At first, I was worried about what I was going to say in my speech, but then when I finally got all the pictures together, the speech wrote itself. This worked wonderfully for me because I did not have to remember anything. Every person in the room gasped when I showed the first slide of me in the hospital. I have looked at this picture for over 20 years, yet still forget how powerful it truly is.

It took me about 15 to 20 seconds to collect myself but then I used the pictures from my PowerPoint to guide me through. I am really glad I had someone record it for me. I do not even remember what I said. It was like I was being divinely guided.

As the weekend was coming to a close for our second book launch, Brenda announced there were some surprise awards that were given by nomination. The first one was the Sacred Hearts Rising Heart-Centered Award!

As Brenda was reading out the letter from the person that nominated the winner, my only thought was, how did I miss that post, I didn't get to nominate anyone. I would have nominated at least two people.

It really was funny as I was sitting at the table listening to her read, I started to think, oh my, I think she might be talking about me, then just as fast as I had that thought my other side kicked in and said, "No, she isn't talking about you."

As she read on, more clues were dropped that she was talking about me. My dear friend Nancy has some special words that she uses to describe me and she put them in the letter.

Then Brenda announced it. The award goes to Daphne McDonagh.

I had no idea I was even nominated and totally taken aback. I did the best I could to keep myself composed but to no avail, I was a crying mess. It was really difficult for me to even see what the award had written on it, but I did the best I could to read out what it said as per her request.

"This individual is caring, compassionate, and willing to help another without looking for something in return. She selflessly gives her time and talents to those in need."

Daphne McDonagh

For one of the first times in my life, I was beginning to see how being kind was actually making a difference.

What do you do to give back while expecting nothing in return?

CHAPTER 22 Transformation

It really is amazing how life works out for us when we know and trust the Universe will always provide.

I love the Quote: If you hang out with me long enough I will brainwash you into believing in yourself and that you can accomplish anything!

~ Rachel Eilene, 2019 ~

This Is how I live my life. I walk with people as they find their magic!

Yes, sometimes life is difficult, but really it is all about our perceptions. I believe when we are given the option of different ways to see things and embrace a new way of being, anyone's world can change. When we release and let go of what is no longer serving us, we can move forward with faith and trust.

In my world the glass is neither half-full nor half-empty, it's always refillable. I think the biggest lesson that I have learned through this whole healing process is that I am never alone and I simply need to ask for help when I need it. So many of us forget that simple step.

It was proven to me again, just the other day, when a new client came to me and shared that she too had a friend that could use some help. He is working on a project that is going to change how society works together for the greater good. My grandma always used to say "Many hands make light work." When we come together one step at a time we can move mountains.

The metamorphic transitions I have gone through are a true blessing. I am aware people's beliefs differ, but I trust in my heart that I actually chose this experience before I got here to bring people together, and that it did.

I cannot even say, "I wish I would have picked something a little bit easier." The minute I realized my worth, I shifted my energy

& started attracting people, situations, and opportunities that respected and reflected who I was and wanted to become.

Sure, I may not have had the typical childhood that many do, but mine was filled with exceptional experiences that others will never get to ever know or understand. At the time, not all of them were all that wonderful, but looking back now, on the flip side of things, I would not want it any other way.

I realize now that I transferred my fate into my destiny simply by the choices I made with the circumstances I was faced with. My blueprint is ever-changing and unfolding now. I am so grateful Spirit is now assisting me to engage in my journey.

What are you most grateful for in your life?

CHAPTER 23 Perspective Is Everything

Who would have thought that a near-fatal car accident would allow me to reach more by sharing the tools that I used to help heal myself? What started as a hobby making magnetic earrings has now turned into my full-time purpose and passion to assist others to navigate the maps of their healing journeys too.

I truly am so happy and grateful every day that I wake up, as it means I still have a purpose to fulfill and I'm aware that everything will work out exactly as it's designed to. I no longer worry about when or how things are going to happen. When I tap into Source and listen, I do not need to think about what is going on.

I love reminding people that in each and every one of them There Is A Healer, A Lioness, A Wild Warrior Priestesses, and a Goddess. Their time as a Caterpillar has expired and it is time for them to find their wings and Be the Beings that they were Born to Be.

This shift in consciousness that is happening right now is the information I learned when I was being bathed in the rainbow colors to receive the light codes. I learned that in order for me to be the best being that I chose to come back to be, I needed to tap into my own intuition and do what I am guided to do. When I stopped following others and what they told me to do, my life got way easier.

Be who you are and say what you feel, because those who mind don't matter and those who matter don't mind. ~Bernard M. Baruch, ~ **n.d.**

It fills my heart with such joy when I can ignite people's imaginations about what is possible so that they can find the motivation to do more with their lives. I know that I can not help everyone, but I can help someone and I want to be the change for that one person that is ready.

I am so happy and grateful that I now get to be a rehabilitation and wellness practitioner who helps animals and people find the sparkle in their eyes again.

If you are the sum of the 5 people you are spending the most time with, take a look around you and choose wisely. I have learned the Universe is abundant and has infinite possibilities.

"Most of the successful people I've known are the ones who do more listening than talking." ~ Bernard M. Baruch, ~ **n.d.**

Today can be the first day of your new beginning if you make the choice to see the flip side. I'm excited for what new adventures present themselves to me each and every day.

Who are your five people that you spend the most time with?

CHAPTER 24 Self Love

Repeat after me:

I Am Blessed.

I Am Grateful.

I Am open to the many wonderful opportunities the Universe is presenting to me.

I now only concern myself with the present moment. I don't worry about the past because there is nothing I can do to go back and change it. All I can do is learn from it and move forward. As for the future, it only matters what I am doing in the present moment that will determine my future.

I realize that only I can make choices for myself, others may have their suggestions or recommendations, but it is me that has the final answer in what I do. Spirit sends me messages in a few different ways. One of the ways is through numbers and another way is through songs.

On the morning of July 17, 2020, at 4:44 am they woke me with the song, "Live, Love, Laugh", by Moccasin Creek & Colt Ford playing in my head. Curious about what they were trying to tell me, I decided to pull up and listen to the song on YouTube.

After hearing the song, I discovered that it was basically telling me to enjoy every moment and have a good time doing it. It reminded me that sometimes life is hard and really sucks, but if I stand up and stay strong, I will be able to get through anything.

It also reminded me that it really doesn't matter how much money I have when I come to the end of my life. The only thing that really matters is how I have treated people throughout my life. When I leave the planet, I want to leave a lasting impression of love.

Yes, the message came through loud and clear. I am glad I was listening.

You Do You, Daphne!

Chill out and have some fun

We Got This!

What are you going to do for you today?

CHAPTER 25 Compassion Is Always A Choice

I focus on what I prefer and leave the rest. Really, the bottom line is when I stopped chasing everything and tapped into my inner self to listen to what I needed, my heart opened and my world lit up.

When I allowed what is, the Universe brought back my happiness.

When I am grateful for what I have, the Universe always brings me more things to be grateful for.

Our bodies are our best healers and when we can sit with ourselves to be ourselves, we do not need anything else to take care of us but ourselves.

We do not need more things.

We need love, not things.

We all are gifts from the Universe.

We do not meet people by accident, there is always a purpose.

If we choose to stay where we are and not change our circumstances, everything will stay the same.

I Live in Gratitude every morning!

I found these two amazing Abraham Hicks meditations to start my day and they really helped me to focus on me and what I needed. These both really inspired me to reach for more. I hope you enjoy them too.

Everything is always working out for me and Good Morning Rampage of Appreciation which can be found on their website:

All of the material is by Abraham-Hicks, © by Jerry & Esther Hicks, the name of the publication from which the material used was excerpted, the AbrahamHicks.com website, and the contact phone number, (830) 755-2299.

These have both helped me immensely to shift my attitude when I am feeling a little off. I also enjoy sharing them with people that come to see me for energy work sessions.

What is your favorite thing to do to start your day off on a positive note?

CHAPTER 26 Don't Blink

The Universe gives us what we are ready for

For me; time, growth, and patience helped me to see what I was asking for. I needed to follow all of the steps along the way to appreciate the journey. Living in the present moment got me to where I am today.

Everything in life is a choice. I feel so blessed but now I can retrace my steps from the past to see the perfection in the way reality has been created in my life. I can now move forward with conviction, all is well now and always will be. I have always done the best I can with what I had. When I knew better I did better.

I like to go with the philosophy that your habits make you what you are. I stay committed to my goals. With steady progress, I will get results. I know it could take a lifetime for me to be an overnight success, so I'm not rushing into anything or burning myself out.

When I am consistent in my words and actions, I know I will build a reliable platform. I am the person someone can count on in a difficult situation. My past has shaped my present and the present is helping me shape my tomorrow.

Acts of love, hope, and mindfulness all shine light on my past and transform my today into a brighter tomorrow. The seeds that I have planted today will blossom and bear fruit. My positive thoughts and actions have planted a blessed future. It is never too late to make a choice to change my direction. All of my answers are within.

As the message from Sandra Kunz's,

The Messenger Cards deck says, "Life is Simple"

Life is simple and yet we insist on making it complicated.

Being present with our feelings and listening to what our soul is asking of us in this moment is about as complex as it needs to be.

We just need to get out of our own way to enjoy the simplicity of this life we have the pleasure of living.

Having fun is essential for taking us out of the past and the future and bringing us into the present moment.

If you're not having enough fun in your life, it's time to examine what you're giving your time and energy to, and make some adjustments.

Our creator abundantly supports us having fun.

Our outer worlds are reflecting our inner worlds.

Every time I hear "Don't Blink" sung by Kenny Chesney, I cry tears of joy.

It was written by Chris Wallin and Casey Beathard, September 13, 2014

I love how this song makes me stop and appreciate life. It totally takes me back to when I was a little girl, running around in the field without a care in the world. Then poof, I was in school. I can remember when I was young and thinking about how long it was going to take to get through school. I never thought I would ever have to relearn how to walk and talk again. I feel so blessed everyday to be able to wake up and get out of my bed independently. I remember when I couldn't do that. Life is such an adventure when we allow it to be. I am so grateful for every step I have had along the way.

It truly is amazing how fast life goes. I was talking to my dear friend Cynthia about when we were younger and she told me the story about how she can remember leaving the hospital at 21 as a single mom, and having no idea what she was going to do.

She told me she got home and placed the car seat on the floor in front of her while she cried buckets of tears and told her newborn son that she had no idea what she was doing but she promised him she would do the best she could. He is now a successful adult and one day hopes to have a family of his own.

What are you going to do today to take a moment for yourself?

CHAPTER 27 Just Do It

I am forever grateful for my dear friend Alli who designed shirts that say,

"Lead With Love." That is how I live my life now. One step at a time with open arms and love to the opportunities that continue to present themselves to me daily.

It truly is about Breaking Free from the confines of what others think and say. When I can stand in my authenticity and shine my light, I will inspire someone else to do the same and the world becomes a brighter place, one person at a time.

There have been many times in my life when I am helping others and they have helped me just as much. For example, I had clients who were dealing with some difficult situations in their lives and as I walked with them on their healing journey we became dear friends. It is so wonderful when we have people in our lives with whom we can share our gifts.

Don't be afraid to meet new people and try new things. You might just be surprised at what sparks your fire and opens your eyes to new possibilities. I never would have thought I would love going to different markets in different cities and provinces to sell my custom crystal creations, yet I am forever grateful for these wonderful experiences.

Not only did I drive independently across two provinces to get to an event, but I am now blessed to have lifelong friends I never would have met had I not said yes to going. Start saying yes to you. You never know what opportunities will show up.

I am so ready for the new chapter that is starting in my life. Remembering that life is an adventure and when I do, I have fun. It is going to be great. It is time to enjoy your life too. It's time for change. Go for it!

I really am so very grateful for all of the amazing people in my life. Like my dear friend Sandra Kuntz who is an amazing artist and has a beautiful soul. As I mentioned earlier, she created an amazing Deck called The Messenger Cards. Whenever I am feeling like I am having trouble seeing the forest through the trees, I like to pick a card as I ask the Universe for Guidance.

On this particular morning, I was sitting in quiet reflection as I chose the Evolution card. Allow me to share this beautiful message with you now.

"We are spiritual beings here to realize our full potential, and the amount of growing room we are willing to give ourselves determines the amount of personal growth and expansion we experience. We are currently in the midst of a large shift of consciousness, and now is a time of opening awareness and increasing energy which is here to facilitate our evolution.

The hummingbird and jaguar represent the male and female energy within us and are there in harmony and balance with each other. As they gaze at each other they experience themselves as two separate beings and yet are intrinsically connected. This represents one aspect of our evolution: collectively and individually, the male and female energy is evolving into one balance and deeper connection. Infinite compassion and space is required to allow the shift to take place. Men and women alike can hold space for these evolving energies to take their new form within us and to experience how they affect us personally and in our relationships. As some of the old paradigms of male and female roles dissolve, many of us may experience the feeling of being lost, displaced, or we may be unable to relate to others in the same way. we can, however, trust that the Universe has a much bigger plan - one that we momentarily cannot see. The more compassion, trust, and space we can hold, the smoother and easier this transition and evolution will be."

Such a perfect message for each and every one of us. We are exactly where we are meant to be at any given point and if we are not happy with our life's situation we can choose to shift and make a change.

What changes are you going to make in your life to see it more like an adventure than a chore?

CHAPTER 28 Guidance

My friend Laura Lee Harrison posted a picture taken by Gabriela Cruz Photography with some beautiful Affirmations that I am now saying every morning when I wake up and every night before I head to dream land.

- I Matter
- I Love Myself
- I Am Worthy
- I Am Valuable
- I have great purpose
- I radiate beauty
- I have a gift to give to the world
- I deserve to be happy
- I Am Intelligent
- I Am Growing
- I Am Evolving
- I Am Learning
- I Am creating a better life for myself

Life truly happens whether we want it to or not. I needed to focus on me and what my next move would be. Funny how things always happen at the perfect moment. My dear friend Hailey was drawn to do channeling for me one day while visiting over tea.

She tapped into my guides and they wanted me to know they wanted me to focus on the three stairs in front of me. The three stairs are really about how I look at stuff.

They went on to explain, the first step is where I look behind myself and say, "Who's coming with me because I'm not going to hold anyone's hand anymore?."

I asked them, "Do you want to come with me or not ?" The people who stepped up to the next step showed her they were shedding their coats of the past. My Guides showed her I am literally taking things step-by-step and how I am a direct Channel/Connection to Source.

They showed her that I stepped forward each day and that I learned lessons from those around me. With each step I took, I learned more. What my guides explained to her, is that there are still some shifts in my beliefs that I needed to work through and that I needn't carry everyone's concerns.

My guides realized that there's a lot of people that I have wanted to help and that I have attached myself to them because I wanted to see them raise up. They let me know that if I truly wanted to move forward in helping them awaken to their natural gifts I needed to allow them to learn their lessons on their own and not push them.

The second step is really about calling in my higher self to welcome more aspects of who I am in this lifetime. My guides talked to me about incorporating more self-power, more confidence, and exhibiting this energy. They told me that I will attract people that are meant to come into my life. As my schedule fills up over the next year I will be thanking the Universe.

Then she saw me on this stage literally presenting to the world and touching hearts all over the place. I am meant to touch the people that are shaking their heads and saying they do not know how to do it because they want somebody to tell them. That's when I step in and remind them that they do not have to do it the way I did. I ask them, "What way do you want to do it?" They are shocked that they have never been given that as an option.

I am to help them learn that it is okay to go look within themselves to find the answers.

My guides showed Hailey, when I incorporate more aspects of myself and use my higher self, my energy completely surrounds and protects me. Hailey said she could see the energy circling 10 feet around me.

My guides showed her there has also been a 10-year struggle of finding who I am and finding the place where I fit in. Finding the circle of friends that I was welcomed into was difficult. I had a lot of friends in a lot of different places, but I never really felt like I fit in. I worked really hard at sharing my energy and gifts with people unconsciously, hoping and praying that I would get something in return, but it never did come back my way. So, I decided to take a step back and take care of myself.

I feel so grateful how within the healing circle community there is a sense of hope. They showed her how I want to inspire others to tap into the Divine bodies that they are. I want them to see that if I can share my uniqueness and that if I can be who I am with support, that then maybe they can too.

My Guides showed her that I can and will help others see their uniqueness. I will help them shine their light. They showed her that I am finally finding the people that bring me unconditional love. People that I can literally go to crying and I don't have to apologize. I don't have to worry I can just be Daphne, in that time, in that moment, and I don't have to put a Shield on or mask myself.

My guides literally told her that I am meant to shine my light and lead the way. I am meant to help others learn that they are not too much. I can help people, but the greatest success I will have is showing others how it is ok to be themselves and shine their light.

Over these past 10 years, I saw how I stopped myself and I saw how the belief that I was holding on to about myself has to have shifted. My guides showed Hailey how over the next 10 years, I was going to be cultivating my power of being the divine being that I am and that I was not going to be ashamed of my power or hide it anymore.

I will tell people If they don't like It they can step to the side, but I'm going to live my life the way I am supposed to do. My Guides literally showed Hailey me standing there and saying, "If you don't like it then you need to figure that out and I'm going to live my life." They showed her that I was calling in my higher power and a higher confidence. My guides showed her that yes I am going to help others step into being the beings they were born to be and live the lives they came here to live.

This beautiful song was brought into my life days after Hailey's amazing channeling.

Be a Light is a song recorded by American country music singer Thomas Rhett and featuring guest vocals from Reba McEntire, Hillary Scott, Chris Tomlin, and Keith Urban. It was released on March 30, 2020.

This song reminds me that even when life is hard I need to stand up and stay strong. I need to be the beacon - like a lighthouse for others to find their way through the darkness.

It helps me to see that we are all one and when we come together to help each other, things can and do shift. When we can all see the bigger picture and lift each other higher, life is so much more fun.

This song reminds me that I need to keep doing what I am doing and not waiver. It let me know that I need to trust my intuition and know that everything is coming together exactly as it is meant to and at the perfect time. I need to shine my light bright so that others can feel safe to do the same.

What are you doing to shine your light today?

CHAPTER 29 Getting Me Back

So many people feel that they need to fight to protect what is theirs. For myself, when I stopped worrying about what was going on and allowed the magic to happen; life unfolded for me. Again, I love how the Universe brings us to the perfect places, people and things at the perfect time.

I am so happy and grateful for the beautiful and very talented, "Tiffany Sparrow" in my life. It was like I was in a euphoric time bubble when she came to my house and offered me a shamanic sound healing session in my backyard hammock.

MAGICAL is the only word I can use to explain this experience.

As she was playing the singing bowls that were laying on my solar plexus chakra and singing, I opened my eyes and the sky looked like it had sparkles dancing in it. I have never experienced anything like this before.

What was even cooler, there was a flock of birds congregating and looked like they were dancing to her music. I understand how that can sound a little strange but for me it is honesty like I was back on the other side being bathed in the rainbow colors again.

I knew right then and there that she was the angelic being that I needed to work with next to walk with me as I reconnected to my higher self that I didn't realize I had forgotten. I am grateful she finally decided to release her Hangups to Harmony program so I could say, "Yes" to investing in me and stepping up to the next level.

Tiffany Sparrows, "Hangups to Harmony" program is all about how to use sacred/shamanic sound practices, music, and other meditative healing to help you ditch body image issues and body hate, shame, judgment, and other barriers to self-love in order to reveal more of your authentic radiance and be-YOU-ty!

Each program is unique to the individual that accesses it, so I can only speak from my experience in saying that it transformed my life. I truly could not have chosen a better time to have taken it. It was the perfect time to let go of that which no longer served my highest good. I feel drawn to share with you the releases that we worked through as I walked this next step of my journey.

You know how people say there is a Healer for the Healers……..Her name is Tiffany Sparrow. She was the spark that lit my fire again and I am honored to also be able to call her my friend. My sessions were very powerful and I am forever grateful for how she assisted me to take care of healing that next layer within myself.

For years, I was the one who was helping people to clear their blockages and stuck energies. It was really wonderful to be able to have someone meet me where I was at, to move through what I needed.

Due to her sessions being so individualized there is no possible way that I could ever do them justice attempting to explain each and every moment. There are some themes but where each person goes is completely up to them.

After taking everything into consideration, I realized that the best way for me to share what I got from these sessions, was to tell you what stood out the most for me. Please remember there is no right or wrong way to process this information.

I do highly recommend that you reach out to Tiffany yourself and please make sure to let her know you found her information through me.

I was extremely nervous before the first session. I had no idea what to expect and no clue where we would even begin. I liked that we were doing the meeting via zoom so I did not actually have to go anywhere and I could stay in the comfort and safety of my own home. The sessions always begin with vocals and body movement. I must admit this was pushing me out of my comfort zone because I am not, nor have ever been able to sing. It was exactly what I needed to do for me to get me back.

A couple of my favorite permission and release statements we worked with in my first session were:

- I give myself permission to be both a masterpiece and a work in progress at the same time!
- I now release all negative thoughts, patterns and programs, beliefs, emotions, vibrations and pockets of stuck emotion from my body, my mind, and my energy field NOW.

These statements assisted me to feel lighter and I was drawn to add this gratitude statement after that HUGE release.

I Am Grateful to work with who I want, when I want, and where I want.

It was so rewarding and freeing for me to work through these statements everyday, morning and night. It really felt like I was unpacking a heavy backpack that I had been carrying for far too long.

When Tiffany first introduced me to Sanskrit my mind was blown. It is the classical language of India and the liturgical language of Hinduism, Buddhism, and Jainism. Sanskrit is a light language and the language of yoga.

It is the language that all of the yogic philosophies were originally conveyed through as well as the other religions listed. Sanskrit is known to be a creationary language, meaning the vowel and consonant combinations help to create what they represent, not just refer to it. I found out she has been going to India since 2008 and regularly visits when she is able.

The first phrase she taught me was, "Om Gam Ganapataya Namaha." I was delighted to find out that we call on the archetype of Ganesh to help with obstacles. Chanting this helps us learn from challenges and obstacles so that they can be removed.

It took me lots of practice to get that one right but there are many nights I fall asleep with "Om Gam Ganapataya Namaha" running through my head.

I must admit, it felt so different being the person on the receiving end of things. I do not remember the last time I had that much oxygen go through my body. I really loved how "Om Gam Ganapatya Namaha" sounded every time we sang it together.

I was really grateful that we did this on zoom and I was muted when we first started because Lord knows I was learning how to match her tone and it wasn't very good yet.

Together we said in call response style. I still use these phrases, almost daily, to help me stay on track in my life. As I said before, each session is individualized. I will share a few of mine, and who knows, maybe one will resonate with you.

- I allow myself to be who I am in the presence of others. I give myself permission to honor myself. To love and be loved more than ever before. To Rest and Rejuvenate with deep reverence for myself.
- I now release all negative thoughts, programs and patterns, vibrations & pockets of stuck emotion from my body, my mind and my energy field now.
- I now dissolve and disintegrate any generational beliefs and thoughts from my lineage that say it's not ok to ask for help, and that I am less than if I do not understand or quickly master anything.
- I release all cords of attachment to these people, to all the places, times, and events where I was shut down, silenced, not supported or something similarly in my emotions.

- I call back my spirit from all of the times, places, memories, events, people & other experiences where I was emotionally shut down. I call back my spirit NOW.

It was truly an amazing experience how Tiffany asked me to bring in the different Archangels to help with cutting cords and to bring in the blue and violet lights for healing.

Like I said before, I felt so much lighter and freer after my first session. I did not know what happened but I felt stronger - like I could take on the world. It really was very liberating for me.

I love how there are so many people that do so many amazing things and I am grateful that I get to share their awesomeness with those who are reading this book too. It really is wonderful to be able to share our gifts with the world.

What transformative choices have you made in your life ?

CHAPTER 30 So Hum

So Hum - I Am That I Am Empowering My Emotions

Before our second session, I had no idea what to expect. I was still feeling like I was on a cloud and floating through my days with no worries or concerns about what was going on around me.

After our singing and movement warm-up which seemed to be easier, Tiffany asked me to state, "I will be gentle with myself, I will love myself, I Am a child of the Universe."

She then guided me on a beautiful journey to work with my inner child. The experience was very eye-opening and revealing. It reminded me how truly blessed I was and what a wonderful childhood I had.

Tiffany then guided me in call response style to repeat after her:

- I dissolve any guilt, regrets, and despair thoroughly and completely from my womb, my crown chakra, and the cells of my DNA, NOW.
- I dissolve and disintegrate any intergenerational patterns of withholding emotions and storing them as guilt, making them non-digestible.
- I call back my spirit from any times when I took on others' stuff knowingly and unknowingly.
- I now lovingly release and forgive anytime I was misunderstood & misinterpreted and taken advantage of. I lovingly release any despair, grief, and regret coming from any times I felt misunderstood.
- I am so grateful. I am free, free, free to express myself in ways that bring me joy, fulfillment, clarity, and deep groundedness.

At the time and to this day, these statements felt so empowering to me. Anyone who knows me knows that I always choose my words carefully. Again, I felt so grateful I was being assisted to see the trees through the forest.

I felt so blessed when Tiffany began singing her song, "Living in the Heart." I do not know if this is something she does for everyone, but I was grateful to hear the words of this song.

When we're living in the heart
Ya we are living in the heart
When I open up my mind there's no more answers left to find
When we are living in the heart
As the years go by there is one that's clear, all I see in you is me too.
You're my mirror
Talk is cheap
Until I'm learning to be rearranged as the change I want to see
No use trying to resist the world outside
To stand for freedom means we can't run and hide
But we're strong together more than when we're apart
So we don't have to go back to the start
When we're living in the heart
Yes we are living in the heart
When I open up my mind there's no more answers left to find
We are living in the heart

I am forever grateful for how Tiffany helped me see things. From that moment, I made a promise to myself to re-evaluate how I see myself. I chose to let go of the old, negative thoughts and self-limiting beliefs. I chose to begin from a fresh place and choose to see my life Anew.

I chose to give myself another chance in life to treat myself with kindness, compassion, forgiveness, and love.

What are you going to do today to treat yourself with kindness, compassion, forgiveness, and love?

CHAPTER 31 Om Krim Maha Kali Sarva Rogam Nasi Nasi

Om Krim Maha Kali - Activating energy of the archetype of Great Mother Kali with her seed sound (Krim)

Sarva Rogam Nasi Nasi - Get rid of all disease, delusion be eliminated, destroyed. It works on shifting the karmic imprint of disease and delusion

Author Unknown

Shared by Sri Sakthi

Original author unknown. Some would say the Divine is the author and it was perceived by some ancient Indian sage several 1000 years ago.

Recently, my teacher Sri Sakthi Amma has shared it with our community to chant regularly.

I was fascinated by this new language I was learning and all of the true meanings behind the words. I loved how Tiffany started all of my sessions.

We called on our soul and our Divine spark, the supreme being that is within us all.

We called on angels, guides, teachers, and friends who love us unconditionally and are helping us every step of the way, even when it feels crunchy and difficult.

We thank you, thank you, thank you for being here with us.

We, of course, called on all of our ancestors. Those who have navigated this world before us and we called on nature, all of the beautiful elements of earth and water and fire and our space and we asked that the combination of all of this assistance seen and unseen that we might grow into more and more and more liberation, more and more love for self and for humanity and more and more awareness for who and what we really are.

I loved how I was making the conscious effort and choice to dedicate time for myself every week. I was excited to find out what new things I was going to learn and do. For the first time in a very long time, I was taking care of myself first, which was very rewarding. I was surprised how I was even able to start matching Tiffany's tones when we sang together.

We sang in call response form for almost an hour. I could feel more layers lifting as we sang. Exponentially grateful are the only words I can use to explain these statements.

- I now release all negative thoughts, patterns, and programs, vibrations, and emotions that are not mine and not for my highest good.
- I release these through all of my levels, through all time and space.
- I now dissolve and acknowledge all patterns of hiding and avoidance, withholding the truth, and keeping secrets that have kept me from digesting life and my feelings.
- I release any fragments of avoidance, of unpleasantries, and any storing of these energies in my body and energy fields, now.

I love how all of the different aspects of this session worked together to assist me in moving to my next step.

What are you ready to dissolve and release today?

CHAPTER 32 Kali Shakti

Kali Shakti - Shakti is the spark that helps things manifest here in form.

During this week's practice, I found myself really out of my comfort zone because I was focusing on different parts of my body and telling each part how much I loved it. While calling on Kali to help soften and dissolve any patterns of clutter resulting from built-up trauma I have ever experienced through this or any other lifetime.

Please allow me to remind you that each person's one-on-one sessions with Tiffany are completely different and the things I was releasing were completely mine.

- I now choose to unplug from any beliefs In the mass consciousness that are holding me any unnecessary fear, judgment, and contain rules or levels of perfection that don't serve me that are unattainable and unreasonable.
- I release all energy wrapped in old survival habits that try to tell me to be someone I am other than myself, or that tell me I should be something different. I Am Perfect as I Am and I listen more and more to the beat of my own drum.
- I trust, I love myself, I respect and honor myself exactly as I am. I am a child of God and as I realize this more and more. I can extend the same courtesy to everyone in my life.

She then guided me on an epic journey to my inner sanctuary. It was an interesting experience that again, left me feeling very light and free.

I felt so blessed when she taught me this Medicine song.

May all mothers know that they are loved.

May all sisters know that they are strong.

May all daughters know that they are powerful.

The circle of women may live on

Way ha hey ya, Way ha hey ya, Way ha hay ahhh, Way ha hey ya, Way ha hey ya, Way ha hay ahhh

Singing this song lifted my spirits, to what felt like I was above the clouds. I felt so empowered to use my energy purposely and continuously. For the first time in a very long time, I felt I would be able to love, trust, respect, and honor myself exactly as I am. Right here. Right now.

I always felt such a sense of loving calm when Tiffany would thank all of the beings that were there to assist. "Thank you, ancestors, the elements, or higher self and the Divine spark. May these all be for our continued elevation higher and deeper."

This was a very hard process for me to go through, but I am forever grateful we did this. Now, each time I am drying off after a shower, I am thanking each body part as I touch it and tell it how much I love it.

What are you going to do to show your body some love today?

CHAPTER 33 Ahem Prema

Ahem Prema - I Am Divine Love

In this session, Tiffany helped me to invoke my soul and my divine spark.

My heart was always filled with so much love when she would call on any angels, spirit animals and guides, teachers, and friends that wanted to be present and love us unconditionally. They can help us as we continue to move through some of our patterns into more and more space, more and more liberation, more and more love, and contentment. She would acknowledge the natural world and give gratitude to the elements. We acknowledged earth, feeling into the earth. We acknowledged water, sending love to the water. We acknowledged fire, heat, and warmth. We acknowledged air and space. The ether and we asked if we could connect more deeply with the natural world and with our true essence and our true nature, and in so doing we could bring about more wholeness and healing for ourselves, for our ancestors, and for all of our relations. So, all the work we are doing is to benefit ourselves and all of those that we come into contact with. Through divine grace, Let that be so.

I was also grateful to start each session with a general clearing of, "I now release all negative thoughts, polarities, pockets of stuck emotion and all, patterns and beliefs that are not for my highest good. Especially those that are not mine."

On this day we did mirror work and holy cow was that ever difficult. For years I was really good at not looking in a mirror so I would not judge myself.

When I looked into my eyes in the mirror and said, "Thank you! I Love You." I almost started to cry.

It was such a transformational time in my life and I am so grateful for every step. When I was going through all of those magical moments, I did not yet realize how these amazing tasks and messages were being brought into my life at the perfect moment. So many learnings and I was aware that I was only cracking the surface.

If you have made it this far in the book, I have faith some of the stories I am sharing here are resonating with you too.

As I look back now, I ponder the many experiences that I have had in my life and am seeing how I really had no clue about what was going on.

How many times in your life have you felt like there was No way out or No way around a difficult situation? Then, "Just in the nick of time", the perfect solution to whatever was going on in your life finds you, and all is well again.

When I truly learned how to be grateful for every experience in my life, the world of infinite possibilities began to layout in front of me.

I Am Grateful to be Grounded in Love.

I Am Grateful to be Safe and Protected.

I Am Grateful to be Leading with Purpose were the three affirmations that Tiffany I and wrote together at the end of my last session.

I reached out to work with Tiffany and her "Hangups to Harmony" program, because I was in a space of not knowing what to do next and not even realizing it. I needed to figure out how to take care of and love myself again. For so many years, I was giving away my power and looking for validation from others.

She helped me by coming from a place of love and understanding. Tiffany is non-judgmental and spoke from experience while exuding unconditional love to walk with me on my journey. She mentored me by asking many thought-provoking questions to dig deeper within myself.

While working with Tiffany, I learned that I am beautiful just the way I am and that my presence does matter. What I really liked was her welcoming and gentle approach to healing and how unique it was. Tiffany never told me what to do. She simply guided me through different processes I had never experienced before. Learning the Shakti chants was very enlightening and thought-provoking.

I found the experience to be both freeing and empowering. My physical and emotional symptoms shifted to being less judgmental and more confident during and after my sessions working with Tiffany. The result is that I am able to focus on myself. I have gained the ability to not be so all over the place and complete one task at a time.

I now have the capacity to look at my body in the mirror and smile. When I say, "I LOVE YOU" to myself, I actually mean it. I no longer feel the need for validation from others. I would recommend Tiffany and her "Hangups to Harmony" program to anyone who is not happy with themselves and is having a difficult time.

What next steps are you going to take for yourself on your journey of life?

CHAPTER 34 Work Your Light

We live our own beautiful healing journey through our connections with others. My dear friend Nancy Nance came into my life when she was learning to heal from some difficult challenges of her own. The Universe is really funny, it allows people to come in and out of our lives in the strangest ways sometimes.

I am exponentially grateful that we are walking together learning as we go. Her readings always bring joy into my life. I was blessed to receive a beautiful reading from her one day and I am even more grateful she was able to share the knowledge with me, so that I may share it with you.

She taught me that I am a Starseed. I learned that Starseeds are souls with a double mission. We raise our own consciousness and the consciousness of the planet. I am an old soul who has incarnated elsewhere beyond this planet.

Nancy shared with me that Starseeds arrive with a feeling that time is running out and that there is something that we came here to do, create, or contribute. The card confirmed that I am a Starseed and I am being encouraged to answer the call. All I have to do is follow what lights me up. The card showed me that I had been dimming my light to fit in. I have avoided my greatness and this message showed me that it is time that I stop dimming my light. It is time for me to embrace the unique light that I came here to share and to treat my time on earth as a glorious vacation.

What lights you up?

I learned to answer the call knowing that I am divinely guided. Even though at times it is scary and life might not make sense, I need to trust my soul's yearnings. I am living a life beyond what my mind could possibly imagine. Answering my soul's callings is not a one-time thing, rather a lifelong dance. Deep down, I already know what I long for. What my soul yearns for. Her reading showed me that the time is now for me to be the being I chose to come back here to be.

Whatever you are called to do, that is your calling. Don't overthink it. Don't wait for permission. Just say YES. I did. I am and I always will follow my divine guidance. Most of us are waiting for a step-by-step plan before we take the first step but intuition doesn't work like that, it takes faith and courage to answer the calls of your soul and that's why most people don't do it.

Let me remind you, You are not like most people and you can do anything you set your mind to.

You are exactly at the right place to answer your call now. You don't need to know the whole plan. You don't even need to know where it is leading. All you need to do is take the next step. No one has ever had a complete, perfect plan. There is no end destination. There is no right or wrong way to do it and you do NOT need permission from anyone else.

Sometimes the more resistance we have around answering a soul calling, the more important it is to our soul's growth. I was reminded that I was being called to either step forward into growth or step back into safety.

What is your soul calling you to do?

I learned that I filter my own experience through my own projections. When someone reminds me of an unhealed experience, I get triggered. Often, it's an unconscious thing. People and situations can trigger me. They show me my own shadow and my light. The shadows and lights reveal the parts of me that are yet to be accepted, witnessed, or loved.

I began to investigate what experiences or people were currently triggering me? What could they be mirroring back to me? When had I felt like this before?

Could they be opportunities to heal something in me? Or, are they shining a light on something that longs to be witnessed in me?

I investigated the good and bad. There are those who admire me and put me on a pedestal. Why do they admire me? I'm not that special am I?

Wait, I am special.

I have lived through challenges in life and healed. I embraced the courage to heal. I realized that I am attracted to people like me. Souls that have triggers and may not realize that they too are triggered by something in them. Some parts of them still need to be healed. We remain hurt and wounded until we are willing to change.

Who or what is triggering you?

What is it in you that they are triggering?

I learned that I could break the chain of pain in my life and heal ancestral patterns. We all can heal our family line and free ourselves from living the life of our ancestors. I can let go of our old maternal or paternal patterns in my life. We all can heal trauma from the past that is not even ours by observing old ways of being that no longer serve us.

We all carry emotional trauma in our luminous field for up to seven generations back. This is why family patterns can be hardest to break. Often, the patterns are not even ours to begin with. But we do not know another way of being and so we continue playing out the drama. I was reminded that I cannot defeat the darkness by keeping it caged inside of me. We don't know what we don't know until we know.

I learned real fast that I cannot heal another person, but my own healing can cause another person to choose to heal. I looked at my life and decided how I wanted it to be. I investigated the ways of being and patterns that I was ready to free myself from. I looked at what part of my future I wanted to rewrite.

I decided now is the time to shake them off and dream a new future into being. I didn't overthink it. I said, "YES" to me.

What old ways of being from your family line are you ready to let go of?

Nancy's reading was opening up so many windows for me to see things from a new perspective. The cards were showing me my greatest challenge in life was to keep my heart open when I wanted to close it. I learned to let life crack me open and through hurt and loss, I finally knew I could allow what was falling away to fall away.

Strength does not only come from physical capacity, it comes from indomitable will too. I realized that being human is a courageous act and a life well-lived is full of losses and tragedies as much as triumphs and adventures. Wherever you find yourself faced with a difficult moment, know that life is coaxing you to keep your heart open no matter how much it hurts. You never know when you are going to meet the next magical person who is going to help you step up to the next level.

Maybe you are going through a difficult time right now. Instead of cursing the difficulty, see it as the blessing it really is. Be open to the truth that, perhaps, as hard as it may be, there is a grander plan. One day, in the not-too-distant future, you may see it was the one thing that broke you down and cracked you open because the world needs your magic. One day, you will look back and realize the transformation you endured and be blown away by the poetry of life. Everything is going to be OK. Remember fear can keep you up at night but faith makes one fine pillow.

I am so blessed to share my story with you and grateful you are joining me on this journey. I softly smiled as Nancy pulled the last card in my reading, which was the Council of Light. This card reminded me of the divine orchestration of angels that surround me daily and how they are my helpers in the subtle realms.

The Council of Light is a team of benevolent beings who are here to assist the raising of consciousness of the planet. They are here to help you achieve your soul mission, and are guiding you every step of the way.

However, because we live in a world where free will reigns, they cannot help you without your permission. If you would like their assistance, all you need to do is ask. They can help with all kinds of requests — nothing is too big or too small.

Think of them as your personal team of helpers in the spirit realm. They are willing and ready to step in and get to work; what would you like help with? My mind was blown when I realized this was a thing. I am grateful to be able to delegate tasks to them now to free up my schedule.

When I began to talk to the council for clarity and guidance regarding my personal mission, my life shifted even more. I put my requests out and let them get to work. They always come through for me. I focus on the things that I prefer to happen and at the same time detach from the need for them to happen as I prefer. This way they can allow things to fall into place exactly as they are meant to.

This beautiful reading reminded me that there is a team of ascended masters, light beings, angels, and guides that are devoted to raising the vibration of Earth and all humanity.

If you are a Lightworker, it is from the Council of Light that you receive your personal mission. Like a spirit world "United Nations", they want to thank you so much for doing this work and devoting your life to uplifting the planet.

Nancy is an amazing Soul that is magical at whatever she is working on. She can help you recover your joy too. Nancy's strategic "Recover Your Joy" program will help you make your dreams a reality.

I have also been blessed to receive SRT (Spiritual Response Therapy) sessions with her. SRT helped me imagine a world where I can reach my fullest potential. This magical meticulous process researches the subconscious mind and soul records to discover and release hidden blocks to health, happiness, and spiritual growth.

The process helps to clear negatively charged experiences, trauma, conflict, and self-punishment. SRT helps clear self-limiting programs and releases interfering energies. Release yourself of phobias, addictions, and other life challenges. Empower yourself for a higher purpose and find your life purpose. Create more joy. Obtain inner direction and guidance easily and with joy.

Which messages stood out the most for you in your life?

CHAPTER 35 So Many Gifts

The last month of 2020 was an amazing transformational time for me and I am honored to share my experience with you in hopes that there might be something to assist you on your journey. I say this because I had the honor of crossing paths with another magical soul named Jeffery Saunders. I am honored he said, "yes" when I asked if I could share what he does with others. I am also grateful he told me the words to use as I didn't even know where to start.

Spirits Transformational Healing Session and Freeing Your Soul with Jeffery Saunders

The main objective of the two sessions was to remove the energies attached from the past that gave me false beliefs about myself, leading me to not feel worthy within my life now and holding me back from having the greater things to enter my life.

In the first session, Jeff increased the frequency of divine light energy and he let that run through my body in healing layers of lower energy that was attached to me where my inner being couldn't forgive myself or others. He released this in the first session, therefore ending my self-sabotaging behaviors.

In the second session, Jeff healed specific experiences all the way back from my childhood to today's date. He walked me through being able to voice out loud each painful experience. Jeff brought it to the surface so the light from myself and from the angelic beings he brought to the session could heal those experiences with the light.

The next step Jeff took was to go back and rescue my inner child after healing the experiences of shame and guilt that I carried for so many years. This allowed my inner child's light to come forth and live more freely, moving forward with the fullness of love, joy, and happiness. This experience allowed my inner child to express my true being of love and light in life.

In the last part of the second session, Jeff healed my heart space with beings from the angelic realm. He held space for all the pain and suffering that had been stored from the painful experiences I have faced. Jeff told me that other people have had the experience of the archangels holding their hand or shoulder as they can feel it during this session. I, myself, felt such a sense of peace and calm, it was so wonderfully enlightening.

When the sessions were complete, I felt like I was given a new life of freedom, love, and joy.

I was so blessed to have a reading/connection call with Ginette in mid-December. The first thing she told me was, "It is Time to Get Out of the Bathtub."

Touching back to when I was in my coma and being bathed in the rainbow colors. She let me know that it is time to step out and share with the world the gifts I have been given. There is no right or wrong way to do this.

Ginette let me know that I am not supposed to rush things right now. She let me know that I am to write out my story; which I have been avoiding for many years. I did not feel that anyone would want to know my story.

I asked my guides if there was something I needed to know about my blueprint and they chuckled and told her that I have made so many changes in my life that have altered my blueprint and that there is really no way for them to be able to foresee what is going to come to be, as each choice I make shifts the outcomes.

The message that I received from them was, "It is time to do the work and that everything will work out the way that it is meant to." I need to have faith and trust that my guides have my back.

When I asked my guides, "What am I supposed to do?" The only answer I received was, "LOVE." It really is that simple. They told me, "It is time to stop hiding behind others and share my gifts." I am to be the conduit for those who are ready to shift their lives. I am to share the many tools that I have used for myself, to heal my body, with animals and people.

Writing this book has been a fear of mine for many years, but I realize the time is now and in order for me to move forward in my life, I need to take the steps necessary to get there.

Like Mel Robbins says in her book, "Take Control Of Your Life", published February 2019, "What is the next lego block that you can place in the bridge you are building to get to your goals? You don't have to have it all figured out. Just take the next step and the opportunity will present itself. The synchronicities will appear." As you can see from reading my book, I have learned this one first-hand many times.

How many times in your life have you had random things just show up after you have had the thought. Remember the Universe can't help you make your dreams happen if you sit on the couch and don't do anything.

It was such a blessing to take part in a magical winter solstice event with the beautiful Elyse Cathrea & Ginette Biro

Elyse led powerful meditations at the beginning and end of the yoga practice that went along with this event. With her permission, I am sharing it here for you to take in and use as you see fit for yourself.

Elyse is a certified Life & Wellness Coach and Yoga & Meditation Instructor, and intuitive universal magic junkie! As an intuitive, she is passionate about creating an inclusive supportive space for people to reconnect with their truest and highest selves.

Elyse believes we all have the answers inside of us via our highest self and our connection to our guides, and that in times of deep disconnect from what fulfills us we must learn to come back home to ourselves first.

Using an intuitively guided approach, she supports people in shifting from feeling disconnected and stuck, frustrated in life, wondering things like, is this what it's supposed to be like? To feeling excited about creating a life they are deeply connected to. Through your work together, Elyse will connect you with your guides to support ways in which you'd like to see shifts in your life. She provides a supportive space for you to reflect and utilize tools from yoga, meditation, and universal energy, to create a path forward.

Elyse was inspired by and referenced "Tanaz from the website Forever Conscious" https://foreverconscious.com/intuitive-astrology-cancer-full-moon-december-2020

The opening meditation she guided us through before doing the Yoga was:

Basking in the Full moon
Finding our bodies on the floor.
Feel the sensation of the moon over top of you.
Let it go. Let the floodgates open. That's what this Cancer Full Moon whispers to us as we bring to a close the year of 2020.

Cancer is ruled by the Moon, so the Moon shines in its element on this night, big and full for all of us to see. As the Moon returns to its favorite spot in our sky, it is able to express its powers to the fullest.

The Moon represents our emotions, but also what makes us feel safe and secure. It represents our ability to nurture ourselves and to take care of our emotional needs.

So much of our safety and security has been up for evaluation this year, but the Moon reminds us that all is not lost. It reminds us that we always have the power to create safety, comfort, love, and warmth right within this bodily vessel we call home.

We are being called within. We are being called to nurture the home of our soul.

Take time to listen to the needs of your body, heart, and soul. There has been much attention, and even fear, placed on the state of our health this year, so take pause to honor, nourish, and attend to your own well-being.

With that being said. Allowing yourself to hold space and Setting an intention for yourself now. Knowing that we have the power to create safety, comfort, love, and warmth within our home and in our bodies. She asked us to set a supportive intention for ourselves as we moved forward.

Then Elyse Walked us through a blessed Yoga Practice and closed with this thought-provoking meditation:

Bring ourselves back to the floor. Noticing the energy within the body. Finding the body on the floor. Turning your awareness inward to the inviting wisdom within you

Recalling that intention and remembering...

We are being called within. We are being called to nurture the home of our soul.

Take time to listen to the needs of your body, heart, and soul. There has been much attention, and even fear, placed on the state of our health this year, so take pause to honor, nourish, and attend to your own well-being.

If you remember all the way back to the start of the year, on January 10, 2020, we also had a Cancer Full Moon, however, this Full Moon was a Lunar Eclipse and its energy was much stronger.

It is interesting that we opened the year with a Cancer Full Moon and we are now closing the year with a Cancer Full Moon. The difference between then and now, however, is that things have softened, the energies are not as strong, there is this sense that we can rest.

Cancer is the 4th sign of the zodiac, and 2020 was also a number 4 year in numerology. The number 4 represents the home. It represents the heart of who we are and feeling at home within ourselves.

Most of us have spent so much more time at home this year. What has this shown us? What have we discovered along the way?

Chiron, the wounded healer, is also very active under this Full Moon. It supports this idea of allowing the murky water to settle, rather than trying to interfere or "fix" things.

Under this final Full Moon of 2020, Chiron works with the energies to remind us that we don't need to prove ourselves to anyone.

We don't need to hold the weight of the world on our shoulders. We don't need to try, we can just be.

Where are you over-extending or overreaching in your life? Where are you burning the candle too fast or strong? Where are you trying too hard?

Perhaps our true gift is realizing how much we have achieved, how much we have grown, and how much love we have poured into the world.

We very often measure our productivity based on the concrete things we have achieved, but why not measure it on how much we have loved, shown gratitude, and practiced kindness.

The Cancer Full Moon will light the path for the new year. It calls for us to let go of all that is weighing us down and all that feels heavy.

It asks for us to let go of anything we no longer wish to bring with us into this new chapter we are about to begin. It calls for us to let it go, not through struggle or effort but through allowing ourselves to just be.

Allow the waves to crash and fall around you. Allow the waves of your emotions to be washed away back out to sea.

Let the vibrations of the Cancer Full Moon soothe you and free you. Allow the energies of the Moon to guide you to your inner home, where all is safe and all is well.

This was such a transformational experience for me. I felt so blessed and grateful to be there at that time.

I love how the Universe keeps reminding me of how when I let go of people and things that no longer serve my highest good, how magically things come together.

My dear friend, Lady Phoenix, asked me a magical question one day.

She told me to ask myself, "What would bring me closer to my natural state of being happy, healthy, joyous, and free?"

I thought that was a great question and the first thing that I thought of was, "I need to get the heck out of my house because I did not do that yesterday and I am craving fresh air and sunshine."

This then led me off onto another tangent thought, "How often in life am I not doing things that would bring me joy?" Now a bigger picture came to mind, "How often in everyone's lives are they doing the same thing?"

2020 was a magical year for many things. I am most thankful for the growth and transformation I had. With everything that was going on in the world, it allowed me to slow down and really go within to see what was really important.

I realized that even though there seem to be many things that we can not do right now, there are actually way more opportunities for new experiences and ways to complete tasks.

I remember when I used to say, "There is never enough time in a day......." Then we were told we needed to stay home for health reasons. We had more than enough time in a day to accomplish tasks.

As I type the last part of this book, I realize with tears of joy rolling down my face (at 1:11 pm on January 11, 2021) my life is just beginning and the possibilities are infinite.

I see now that there is really no right or wrong way to live life, and I realize that my many amazing experiences have molded me into the person that I am today.

This is why I am so happy and grateful that I went through what I did when I was 15. It allowed me to Un-Become everything that I was not, so that I could come back here and hold space for others to do the same.

The many gifts that I was given while I was blessed to be visiting the other side are being revealed to me more and more now that I am ready to receive them. I am no longer afraid to "Be the Being I Came Back Here To Be." I am embracing the powerful punch of the possibilities for the potential of prosperity that is flowing into my life!

What would bring you closer to your natural state of being happy, healthy, joyous, and free?

What choices are you going to make for yourself to move forward?

CHAPTER 36 A Moment For Meditation

It is wonderful when we live from our truest hearts, how people of the same vibration and message come into and stay in our lives.

I invite you to take a moment to soften your mind and heart and focus on your inner being.

Thank you for being here with me on this journey.

I am honored to connect with you in this way.

May this "I Am" affirmation journey uplift and empower you, to give you exactly what you are needing in this moment.

Now, imagine you are standing somewhere in nature surrounded by Majestic mountains.

Noticing whatever it is that you are noticing about this place. See yourself holding a snow globe in your hands. See the snowflakes swirling and dancing inside of it.

Now, for a moment, imagine that every snowflake represents some negative thought or emotion that has been draining you.

As the snowflakes start to settle one by one, see the globe turning into a colour that represents all of the lower vibrational thoughts and emotions inside of it. Go with the first colour that comes to mind.

Now, throw that snowglobe towards the mountains. By magic, it is carried over them. See it becoming smaller and smaller as it disappears from your site completely.

Take a deep breath in and hold it for a moment. As you release your breath, see yourself standing tall, while becoming steady as the mountains.

Imagine the empowering and loving words I share with you are your words. They are your reality.

Know and trust that your subconscious mind listens and only that which is for your highest good will be absorbed and reinforced into the core of your being.

Activating your true essence now and in every present moment Is the only place you can change.

I am reincarnated in my physical body knowing that I am the master creator of my reality.

I understand that my body always seeks balance and is in flow.

I am grateful to be an instrument of the Universe and to be here to spread love.

With my power I can make choices in every situation I find myself in.

In every present moment, I have the power to create something new.

I am grateful I keep myself open to new experiences.

Feelings of powerlessness and hopelessness are a choice.

Activating my inner strength encourages a choice.

All emotions are vibrations that we as humans create with our own mind.

No one else creates them for us.

We can blame others.

We can blame our past.

We can blame our economy or the weather.

However, going down that path recreates more of the same.

I am grateful for the reminder that my world is a reflection of my thoughts on all levels and the people in my world are reflecting my thoughts back to me.

What I choose is up to me.

How I feel is purely up to me.

All that I experience happens for me, from my higher good.

Life will only give me peace when I create peace within me first.

The Universe can only give me the matching vibration of the frequency that I am.

The vibration I am emitting most of the time during my days, weeks, months, and years is my overall vibration.

My overall vibration creates my reality.

Emotions are teachers.

Emotions are safe.

No matter how positive they are on the ends of the scales, they are just energy.

When I allow myself to stay within them, listening, speaking, acknowledging, and accepting them, I will start to unwrap the portal of learning and healing of all that they hold.

It all comes down to my willingness.

I am grateful to be willing to be vulnerable and feel my emotions.

When I allow myself to fully penetrate each emotion and fully feel them, see them, hear them, and show them compassion, then they will heal and I will release that energy.

Leaving Learning, Love, & Wisdom in its wake.

I am grateful to be a universal conduit of love.

I am grateful to be a soul and a human body.

I am grateful to be here now to learn, to grow, and to experience life to the fullest, being able to embody all the contrasts of life.

I am grateful I choose to be here now in the shifting of the ages to bring love to the planet.

It is time now to create a new chapter in the book of my life.

The chapter where I let go of the illusion of the idea I need to control everything.

The more I try to control, the more I am stuck in the quicksand of low vibrational emotions.

Trust is reaching out to me.

Faith is reaching out to me.

Love is reaching out to me.

I am ready to take this leap of faith now, trusting life from a higher perspective with an open and activated heart.

All challenges are here as opportunities for learning, healing, and expansion

They tell me what I need to hear, the truth that I am holding on to thoughts, beliefs, and events from my past that are ready to be healed and released.

How I am going to transform and heal them is my choice.

This is up to me and this process that I can choose to trust.

It may take time, because time is a part of the alchemy that is needed for our physical reality for change to manifest.

The alchemical process of healing most of all needs to be my willingness to heal and my willingness to take full responsibility for the state of my being, my vibration and my life.

I am worthy.

It is possible to heal and change my circumstances.

From now on, I will take the action steps necessary every day. Step-by-step, small steps, big steps, leaps of faith.

I am willing to work with time and I am grateful to trust the process.

I am willing to step up my game and face all of my challenges with my back straight and chin held high.

I am free to change my thinking and my choices or actions in any situation.

I am grateful to be inviting peace and harmony into my body now.

I am choosing to learn from my emotions and when I am willing to heal and let them go.

To be vulnerable is a strength.

It is bravery. It is honesty. It is authenticity.

It is the path to activate the fullness of love, wisdom, and inner power that is available to me at all times.

I am setting healthy boundaries now. Enough is enough.

My energy, my health, and my well-being is my first priority from now on.

I am grateful to be balancing the scale of giving and receiving.

I am more than good enough.

I am grateful to be kind, loving, and patient with myself.

I am grateful to finally realize that I am pure love and consciousness in the human body.

I chose to honor, love, and respect my human self.

I am learning new things about myself every day.

I love to learn.

I use and infuse my energy on taking care of my body, my mind, and my spirit.

My body is the home of my soul.

I am grateful to be raising my standards and creating rituals that support my well-being now.

I am communicating lovingly with my precious body even if I have not loved and accepted myself fully in the past.

I choose to do that now.

It is safe to allow it to happen naturally. I can take my time.

I am willing to accept myself fully and completely for the highest good of all.

The level of love that I have for myself and my life has a tremendous power that permeates the core of the collective consciousness of humanity. When I choose to love myself, I raise my vibration and thus raise the vibration of the collective consciousness.

Love is always within me.

I am letting go of the need to have an opinion about others.

Unless it's uplifting and empowering, I let it go.

I am aware.

I am awake.

I am alive.

With every moment I sow the seeds for my future.

I am grateful to be activating and opening doors to new realities.

I feel empowered, centered, and secure.

I choose to tap into my subconscious mind now and enact my ability to feel safe and secure in all scenarios that I co-create.

All my emotions are created from within me.

I have access to the whole buffet of emotions that exist.

Today I choose to feel safe and secure. Today I trust and I have faith.

I trust in the Universe.

I am grateful to be trusting in life.

I am grateful to be free to let go, heal, and move on.

Some things may take time to heal and that's ok.

Trusting life is the key that sets me free.

Change is a sign of life.

I choose life.

Self-love, acceptance, and trust are all keys that help me keep connected to the higher path of my soul's purpose.

I choose to cleanse my mind and my physical surroundings of all the things that need to go.

I am grateful to be courageous and confident.

I am embodying these resourceful states now because I can.

I am free to say yes.

I am free to say no.

I am free to follow my heart.

I am free to learn from my past.

I grow from my past.

I choose to be grateful for what I have. All that I experience is serving a purpose.

I am releasing the need to understand everyone and everything.

Other people's opinions are not my business.

Their choices are not my business.

That doesn't mean I have to like it or think that it's OK.

It means that I accept my reality as it is. I am grateful to be detaching from the need for others to understand me 100%.

My human self wants to control life. Trying to control is the opposite of having control.

I am grateful to be optimistic and focused on the future I intend to create. I am focusing on the things that I prefer to happen and at the same time, I am detaching from the need for it to happen as I prefer.

I choose to embody trust.

I am grateful to be embodying trust.

I am trusting my body.

I choose to be grateful for whatever happens.

I always find a solution.

It always works out.

Everything happens for me. I know this deep inside. I see, feel, and hear everything that happens as an opportunity for me and allows others to shine brighter and stronger.

I am grateful for the universal love and wisdom that is soaring through my veins and consciousness at all times. When I am in the present moment, I am grateful to be a full embodiment of love, power, wisdom, and action.

I have a place in this world.

I am important to this planet.

Divine light circulates within me and through me.

I am grateful to be at peace within myself and my life.

I am worthy.

I am deserving.

I am love.

I am grateful for the positive changes that are happening full of love, growth, abundance, and prosperity in my life. All this or something better is happening now in a multitude of realities for the highest good of every soul involved.

In whatever way you choose to show up in your life today, please allow the energy and intentions of this transformative "I Am" affirmation meditation to affect you in the most empowering and positive way.

From my heart to your heart.

From my soul to your soul.

Thank you for your trust.

I believe in you.

I see the light in you.

Shine bright dear soul.

You are safe.

You are loved.

You are protected.

Connect yourself to the Web of light codes to lift you higher.

Share your magic.

I invite you now to be a conduit of unconditionally universal love too. Take one more deep breath in and thank the Universe for the abundance that surrounds you.

What are you going to do to share your magic with the world ?

CHAPTER 37 Final Thought

Let me ask you again, "What if we could spread love as quickly as we spread hate and negativity?" What an amazing world we would live in.

My dear friend Hazel used to read this inspirational quote every day while she was still here on this earth.

This is your life

Do what you love and do it often

If you don't like something, change it

If you don't like your job, quit.

If you are looking for the love of your life stop

They will be waiting for you when you start doing things you love

Open your mind, arms, and heart to new things and people,

We are united in our differences.

Ask the next person you see what their passion is and share your inspiring dreams with them.

Travel often; getting lost will help you find yourself

Some opportunities only come once, seize them

Life is about the people you meet and the things you create with them

So go out and start creating

Life is short

Live your dreams and wear your passion

All emotions are beautiful

When you eat appreciate every last bite

Life is simple!

I feel so blessed to be connected with the many amazing people in my life. I now realize that wherever I go and whomever I meet, there is an invitation to tap into my intuitive senses to get to know them with ease and grace. When I pay attention, I can gauge others' motives, ambitions, and fears, often instantly being able to understand so much about their life situation.

Without always knowing how, I seem to assist others into a new awareness of their life circumstances, opening up the possibility for them to make substantial adjustments in their lives. I don't always appreciate the effects my abilities have on others, nor that others do not necessarily have the same perceptions I do.

I am blessed, grateful, and open to always be in the right place at the right time to cosmically attract magical manifestations into my life.

I realize now that when I engage with people, I need to be clear that I come from a foundation of love and integrity rather than a place of manipulation. I see people and their life intentions quickly now. The mystery of life fascinates me and I will do almost anything to find out "What it's all about."

As a quote from Jari Askins says

"It's not about thinking outside the box. It's about realizing there is no box." **n.d.**

Are you listening to your inner voice?

Are you ready to start living your best life?

Are you willing to do what you need to do for you to allow for your brilliance to shine through?

Allow me to close in saying

YOU DO YOU
AND THE WORLD
WILL ADAPT

Resources from People who Inspired Me

Dr. Sheryl Rist: https://dr-sheryl.business.site/, Chapter 12

Magnetite with Hematite reference website, Chapter 12
http://www.crystalguidance.com/prescriptions.html
- Crystal Therapy Doreen Virtue, Ph.D., and Judith Lukomski
- Healing Crystals Michael Gienger
- The Crystal Bible 1 & 2 Judy Hall
- The Healing Crystal First Aid Manual Michael Gienger

Cynthia Gauvreau: http://www.cynthia.services & www.wandpublishing.ca, Chapter 12

Abraham-Hicks: http://www.abraham-hicks.com/, Chapters 17, 25

This material is by Abraham-Hicks, ℗ by Jerry & Esther Hicks, the name of the publication from which the material used was excerpted, the AbrahamHicks.com website, phone number, 1-830-755-2299

Mesmerica: https://www.jameshood.com/mesmerica, Chapter 17

Alli MacKenzie: https://linktr.ee/alli_the_clarity_coach, Chapter 18

Ginette Biro: https://avalonspirit.com/, Chapters 19, 20, 35

Christina Marie: https://www.instagram.com/createdwithloveinc/, Chapter 21

Sandra Kuntz: https://www.strokeofsoul.com/, Chapters 26, 27

Tiffany M Sparrow: https://www.tiffanysparrow.com/, Chapters 29 to 33

Nancy Nance: http://exponentialjoy.com/, Chapter 34

Jeffory Saunders: www.thecanadianhealingmedium.com, Chapter 35

Elyse Cathrea: https://avalonspirit.com/collections/personal-journey-guides/products/personal-journey-guide-elyse-cathrea, Chapter 35

About the Author

Daphne McDonagh is a Rehabilitation & Wellness Practitioner, Intuitive Healing Energy Coach, Universal Sphere Practitioner, Animal Communicator, as well as a Crystal and Cold Laser Therapist.

Daphne received her Rehabilitation Practitioner Diploma from Grant MacEwan University in 2000. She also holds a Diploma in Animal Sciences from the International Career School of Canada and a Healing with Crystals Diploma from the Universal College of Reflexology.

She is an International Best-Selling Author for Sacred Hearts Anthology, a Public Speaker who has been interviewed on various international podcasts and shows, and has been published in national magazines. Daphne has been facilitating healings for animals and people for over 20 years and has clients all over the globe. She is honored to offer in-person and distance healing energy work for animals and people that are committed to healing themselves.

Daphne is truly honored to share her experiences with you to lift you higher and to share the message of when "You Do what works for You", life is a magical place to live.

Author's Publications

Sacred Hearts Rising: Breaking the Silence One Story at a Time

Sacred Hearts Rising: Finding Your Wings

22065851R00085